JANUARY

GW00871195

Buist Glory 15.6

VOLUME 15 / PART 1

Edited by **Grace Emmerson and John Parr**

>> The Bible Reading Fellowship
OPENING THE BIBLE

Writers in this issue

1 and 2 Thessalonians **Jonathan Knight** is Research Assistant to the Bishop of Ely, and author of several books on the New Testament..

Isaiah 1–39 **Michael Thompson** is a Methodist minister, serving as Superintendent of the Bishop Auckland Circuit in County Durham. He is involved in the training of Local (Lay) Preachers, and recently published a book on the Old Testament and prayer, *I Have Heard Your Prayer.*

The Glory of the Lord **D.E.R. Isitt** is a retired priest of the Church of England who has worked in Cambridge as a parish priest and as a college chaplain, and in Bristol as Director of the Diocesan School of Ministry.

John 13–21 **John Parr** is priest-in-charge of Harston with Hauxton and Newton, near Cambridge, and Continuing Ministerial Education Officer in the Ely Diocese.

The Song of Songs **Stephen Dawes** is Chairman of the Cornwall District of the Methodist Church. Formerly he taught Old Testament and Hebrew at Trinity College, Legon, Ghana and at Queen's College, Birmingham.

Psalms 120–134 **Michael Tunnicliffe** is Director of Studies for the Northern Ordination Course. He previously served as a Methodist minister in Stoke-on-Trent and Birmingham. He is currently writing a volume of 1 and 2 Chronicles, Ezra and Nehemiah for the BRF commentary series, *The People's Bible Commentary*.

THE BRF
Magazine

The BRF Prayer

O God our Father,
in the holy scriptures
you have given us your word
to be our teacher and guide:
help us and all the members of our Fellowship
to seek in our reading
the guidance of the Holy Spirit
that we may learn more of you
and of your will for us,
and so grow in likeness to your Son,
Jesus Christ our Lord.
Amen.

Editors' Letter

A happy new year to Guidelines readers, as we begin the final year of the second millennium. Once again, the readings for the next four months bring out the variety and richness of the Bible. We shall be reading brief and insistent letters to hard-pressed churches (1 and 2 Thessalonians), a long and complex collection of prophetic material (Isaiah 1–39), passages collected from different parts of the Bible around the theme of glory, passionate and evocative love poetry (Song of Songs), the second half of John's Gospel, and selections from a collection of hymns used by Jews and Christians for over two millennia (Psalms of Ascent). In different ways, this biblical material reminds us that God's ancient word is always new and relevant, with something fresh to offer to every generation.

It is always good to welcome new writers to Guidelines. From the Ely Diocese (at the time of writing), Jonathan Knight draws out the hopeful message of 1 and 2 Thessalonians, without shirking some of the difficulties of reading material from a world whose basic assumptions are so different from our own. Michael Thompson from County Durham guides us through Isaiah 1–39, helping us to hear the prophet alerting his contemporaries to the holy God whom they profess to worship. David Isitt, now retired in Cambridge, shows how the most important narratives of the Bible—the stories of exodus, exile and Jesus—shed light on the glory of God. The fine love poetry of the ancient Song of Songs comes alive as a moving celebration of the delights of human love, and as an allegory of God's love for us, challenging us to respond. The poetry of love prepares us for the most poetic of the gospels, as we conclude our readings in John's Gospel with the vision of God's glory and love in the passion and resurrection of Jesus. Fittingly this issue finishes on a note of worship, with the Psalms of Ascent. Coming as they do from the hymn book used by Jews and Christians over many centuries, they are read from four different perspectives: a pilgrim in the years before and after the exile in Babylon, a worshipper in Jesus' time, and finally a modern-day Christian.

Please continue to support in prayer our worldwide fellowship of readers, contributors and editors, that we may all go forward in Christ's service with renewed strength and faith in this new year.

With all good wishes.

Grace Emmerson, John Parr
Guidelines Editors

Richard Fisher writes...

Happy New Year from all of us at BRF. At the time of writing (June 1998) it is remarkable to think that it is almost a year since the death of Shelagh Brown, *New Daylight*'s Commissioning Editor for nine years. Looking back over this past year we marvel at the way in which God has provided for us in BRF in so many ways, and has brought new people into the BRF team to continue the work. Once again, thank you for your prayers for us all—we are very conscious of being upheld in prayer by so many people throughout the world. And we pray for you as we meet each morning as a staff team in Oxford.

BRF book publishing

Our book publishing programme is now firmly established alongside the regular series of Bible readings notes. Our adult publishing is divided into Advent and Lent, Prayer and Spirituality, and Bible Reading and Study, and our ranges for younger readers include the Barnabas imprint for children under the age of 11, and a range of resources for 11–14s and their youth leaders. Overall, our book publishing explores the twin themes of the Bible and Prayer, which are at the heart of BRF and its vision, and of course at the heart of our discipleship as Christians. If you would like to see a copy of our new adult and children's catalogues, send an A4 38p s.a.e. to the BRF office in Oxford. And if you would like to receive regular information about new BRF resources, write and let us know.

A fresh look at the teaching of Jesus

Message for the Millennium

One of our most important books for the first half of 1999 is *Message for the Millennium*, our new Lent Book by David Winter. David is well known as Editor of *New Daylight* and as a regular broadcaster on BBC Radio. He has written several books for BRF, including our best-selling Lent Book in 1995 *What's in a Word?* In his new book David takes a fresh look at the teaching of Jesus. What better way for us as Christians to prepare for the Millennium than by re-examining the teaching of Jesus, without whom the Millennium has no meaning? You will find information about the book, and an extract, on page 14.

Subscription rates

We have decided to maintain the current group and individual subscription rates for the new subscription year beginning 1 May 1999 (see page 155 for details). If you would like to give someone a gift subscription to BRF notes, you will find an order form on page 156.

The BRF Magazine

In this issue of *The BRF Magazine,* Brother Ramon offers a further article on prayer, this time exploring *The Jesus Prayer and healing.* We have received many letters of appreciation concerning his earlier articles and Bible reading notes in *New Daylight* and are delighted to say that he is currently writing a book for BRF as well. John Fenton continues his series on *The Lord's Prayer*, this time examining the phrase 'And forgive us our

The Bible, the written word … the living word, Jesus Christ

debts…' and Colin Bennetts, Bishop of Coventry and Vice-Chairman of BRF's Council of Trustees, offers his thoughts on the continuing significance of the Bible for our Christian lives as we approach the new Millennium, in an article, 'The Living Word'.

In addition there is a profile of Rob Gillion, who has recently begun writing for BRF as a new contributor to *New Daylight*, and an interview with Brian Ogden, author of the *On the Story Mat* series for 5–6 year olds.

We do hope that you will find this issue of *The BRF Magazine* to be of interest and that you will enjoy the Bible reading notes themselves. Please do keep sending us your comments and feedback. We value this greatly and are grateful for the many readers' letters we receive each week.

And finally

As we look to the approaching new Millennium, let's pray that there will be many who discover the Bible, the written word, and through it encounter the living word himself, Jesus Christ.

The Jesus Prayer and healing

Brother Ramon SSF

Some months ago, Bishop Simon Barrington-Ward visited me in my hermitage. We had not met previously, and we experienced such a gift of exhilaration and joy that has been quietly bubbling in our hearts ever since. The reason for our meeting was that we had both written books on the Jesus Prayer*, and we wanted to share some of our evangelical and contemplative experience of the love of God in further exploration.

The Jesus Prayer is simple and biblical. It is rooted in two incidents in the eighteenth chapter of Luke's Gospel. The first is the story of the tax collector who, feeling his unworthiness, cried out in repentance, 'God, be merciful to me, a sinner' (v. 13). The second is the story of the blind man at Jericho who needed healing, and cried out persistently and savingly, 'Jesus, Son of David, have mercy on me' (v. 38). If you put these two attitudes of repentance and faith together, the result is the Jesus Prayer:

Lord Jesus Christ,
Son of God,
have mercy on me,
a sinner.

When I first followed the Lord's call, laying aside my frenetically busy life of evangelism and ministry, I went with a small unheated caravan for three years in the middle of the country. Halfway through, in a particularly cold December, I suffered a sudden attack of extreme vertigo and high blood pressure, in which I had to pause and take stock. There was tremendous joy in living the life of prayer and solitude in God, but I needed to regulate the asceticism! One of the main things that came out of that period was the way in which the Lord led me to open up my mind and body to his healing love.

Christians do get sick, and physical healing is not always the consequence of prayer and faith. I say this because of the danger of Christians feeling that if they are not healed, it must be the result of either backsliding or lack of faith. This produces guilt, which is an added burden to the illness they are already coping with. I want to share with you the way in which your mind and body can be opened up to the receptive attitude in which God can and will bestow his grace. This may well mean physical healing as well as spiritual illumination.

Prayer for healing

The Jesus Prayer has to do with salvation, and salvation is for the whole person. As I continued to use the Jesus Prayer each early morning, I found myself developing a fourfold variation of the prayer which was specifically aimed at healing of body and mind. Once learned, it has an immediacy of appeal for whenever the need arises. I shall now describe it, and then expound its relevance and meaning:

1. Lord Jesus Christ / Son of God, let your healing flow down / upon me.

2. Lord Jesus Christ / Son of God, let your healing spring up / within me.

3. Lord Jesus Christ / Son of God, let your healing love / enfold me.

4. Lord Jesus Christ / Son of God, let your healing power / flow through me.

The Jesus Prayer has to do with salvation

This is not a begging prayer, persuading a reluctant God to answer a desperate plea. Rather, it seeks to bring the believer into an attitude of expectant receptivity, so that the healing power of God may flow into the whole person. It links the believer with the fountain-head of creative love. If sins are forgiven, and the believer is receptively open to the Holy Spirit, then the river will flow into the dry and dark places of the soul. Now let us look at the meaning of these prayers.

1. 'Let your healing flow down upon me.' This is directed to Christ the Saviour who gazes into the believer's heart. It is the image of the healing Jesus who lays his hands upon the leper, and whose power flows from the transcendent source of light and love.

2. 'Let your healing spring up within me.' Here is the acknowledgment that your body is the temple of the Holy Spirit, awaiting the rising spring of the healing and restorative powers that already reside within. This prayer is directed to the immanent Christ, the interior, indwelling mystery which is the hope of glory (Colossians 1:27). The image is a quiet, bubbling, healing spring which, when the rubble is cleared away, will flow into every crevice of your being.

3. 'Let your healing love enfold me.' If Christ is transcendent *above* you, and immanent *within* you, he also completely *surrounds* you, enfolding, caressing, as a protected child is enfolded within the loving embrace of its mother. This is not a negative regress to the womb in fear of a wicked world, but rather a conscious retreat into the divine Love, so that, sustained and restored, you may return to the world nourished and transformed.

4. 'Let your healing power flow through me.' You must not become a stagnant lake with no outlet. Love always flows, and you are the channel of its communicative grace. If you experience the forgiving, healing power of God's peace, then you will be the channel of its flow to other lives. Where the river flows there will be fertility and fruitfulness.

Return to simplicity

On first reading, this practice may sound complicated, but if you read it through slowly and prayerfully, it will soon become clear. Write out the four prayers boldly on card, placing them before you until you are completely familiar with them, then the whole process will become easy and natural. Here is a simple pattern:

- Find a quiet place
- Sit or kneel (in loose clothing), relaxed, yet alert
- Let your breathing become gentle, regular, as you breathe in the presence of the Holy Spirit
- After a few minutes of stillness, begin gently to repeat the first prayer three times
- Continue with the other three prayers and, if you feel led, repeat the sequence, leading into silence
- When you feel it right, conclude with the Gloria: 'Glory to the Father and to the Son, and to the Holy Spirit; as it was in the beginning, is now, and shall be for ever. Amen.'

Love always flows, and you are the channel

If you find this practice productive, you may like to continue it in the context of the Jesus Prayer, and even join a Jesus Prayer group, developing it in your own way. May it lead you into healing and renewal of body, soul and spirit (1 Thessalonians 5:23).

* Simon Barrington-Ward, *The Jesus Prayer* BRF.

  Brother Ramon SSF, *The Heart of Prayer* HarperCollins

A profile of
Rob Gillion

We welcome Rob Gillion to the regular team of *New Daylight* contributors. He wrote the notes for the current issue while he was still serving in Hong Kong, where he has been on the staff of the parish of St John's cathedral since 1990, but during 1998 he came home to England to take up the post of Officer of Evangelism for the Bishop of Kensington.

Rob trained at Drama School in London and worked as an actor and director for ten years. He was ordained in 1983, serving his curacy in Norfolk (at East Dereham) and then on the staff of the Richmond parish team, before going out to Hong Kong with his wife and family in 1990. In Hong Kong he helped to plant a flourishing, multi-racial congregation at Discovery Bay on Lantau Island, became chaplain to the high security Shek Pik prison, and eventually was in charge of religious broadcasting for Radio & Television Hong Kong. During the tense time of the handover of power to the Chinese, Rob was for a time Acting Dean of the cathedral, and shared in a number of important broadcasts, including the *Songs of Praise* from the island prior to the

transfer, and a *Thought for the Day* on Radio 4 on the day itself. He is already a familiar voice to many radio listeners in Britain, having contributed frequently to *Prayer for the Day* on Radio 4.

As *New Daylight* readers will discover, Rob has a great appetite for life! With his wife, Janine, who also trained at drama school, he believes that the Christian faith is intended to be life-enhancing, not dull and dutiful. But his experiences in Hong Kong, not least in ministering to the miserable 'Boat People' for many years, and in the prison, have given him a perspective and experience denied to many of us in the West. As his family settle back in the UK we are delighted to welcome them into the BRF family!

And forgive us our debts, as we also have forgiven our debtors

John Fenton

The apostle Paul reminds his readers in Rome, 'We shall all stand before the judgment seat of God' (Romans 14:10). This was part of the faith that he and they and all the believers shared. They looked forward to the future with confidence and joy: they longed for it to happen and prayed that it would take place soon.

One of the reasons why they had such a positive attitude to the future was that they believed they knew who would be their judge on the last day. We can see this, if we look at another passage in Paul's letters, where he mentions the same future event: 'All of us must appear before the judgment seat of Christ, so that each may receive recompense for what has been done in the body, whether good or evil' (2 Corinthians 5:10).

The one who will sit on the judgment seat of God is Christ; but he is the one who has died for us and now intercedes for us; he has associated us with himself; we are his brothers and his sisters, his bride, the members of his body. We can therefore look forward to the future with confidence.

Christ is the one who now intercedes for us

This is the context in which the first followers of Jesus said the Lord's Prayer. They longed for God to make all things new: to hallow his name, to rule the world and to make his will effective over all opposition. They asked God to give them the bread of the age to come and thus make them participators in the good things that he had prepared for them. And they dared to ask for their sins to be forgiven at the judgment to come, an inevitable part of the transition from the present to the future. Hence the petition that follows the prayer for the bread, 'And forgive us our debts, as we also have forgiven our debtors' (Matthew 6:12, NRSV).

The original Lord's Prayer will have been spoken in Aramaic, the language of Jesus and his disciples. We do not have the original wording of the prayer; we have translations into Greek, in Matthew's Gospel and in Luke's; and it is possible that they are independent translations of the Aramaic original.

In Aramaic, one word could mean both 'sin' and 'debt'. One can see how this came about: if we think of ourselves as under obligation to our Creator, then we owe him obedience, and all disobedience is debt.

Matthew uses the Greek word that means 'debt'; what he writes could be translated: 'Cancel our debts as we have cancelled the debts that are owed to us.' Luke, on the other hand, combines the two ideas (sin and debt) in his translation: 'Forgive us our sins, for we ourselves forgive everyone indebted to us' (Luke 11:4). (The difference between Matthew and Luke here may be the result of their writing for different audiences—Matthew for Jews, Luke for Gentiles.)

The parable of the two debtors (Matthew 18:23–35) sets out very clearly the relationship between forgiving and being forgiven. Those who have observed the behaviour of the man who was let off the vast debt of ten thousand talents (something like the total annual tax bill for a province in the Roman Empire) are horrified at his demand for payment of the much smaller sum, and his decision to put his fellow servant in prison. The appeal is to what should be obvious to any fair-minded person: 'Were you not bound [morally] to show mercy to your fellow servant just as I showed mercy to you?' It was an offence against what is expected in any decent society.

We remember this parable, as we say the Lord's Prayer, and we acknowledge the indissoluble relationship between being forgiven and forgiving. If what we need is remission of a vast debt that we owe to God, we are in no position to insist that anyone owes us anything. We do not have the standing that would be necessary in order to make such a claim. It would be completely inappropriate for those who have been bankrupt themselves, and then let off, to pursue other people for any small sums owed to them.

If we see ourselves as followers of Jesus, we have to abandon honour and status; we cannot appeal to justice for ourselves, but ask God for mercy. The measure that we ask him to use in his dealings with us must be the same measure that we use in our dealings with one another (Matthew 7:1, 2). Anything else would be hypocrisy (Matthew 7:5).

We cannot appeal to justice, but ask God for mercy

Message for the Millennium

David Winter

Many Christians are concerned that the Millennium celebrations are in danger of leaving out the only reason that we have to celebrate at all—the birth of Jesus Christ. As Christians, giving Jesus his rightful place in the celebrations is our responsibility, but how confident are we that we know what he actually taught? Many people know the story of Jesus' life, but the wisdom and challenge of his ethical, moral and spiritual teaching are often lost, even to many of those who claim to be his closest followers.

David Winter has grasped the challenge and presented it in the form of forty daily readings which focus on the teaching of Jesus, with nothing added but explanatory background and reflective material. He has made the teaching of Jesus accessible to the modern reader.

David says, 'Although the material is arranged under forty headings, the book did not start with a list of topics for which I then tried to find relevant passages from the gospels. In fact, the procedure was precisely the reverse. I went through the three 'synoptic' gospels (Matthew, Mark and Luke), noting every part of the teaching of Jesus as it occurred and 'filing' it under categories. From an examination of those categories I was able to assemble what I believe

Teaching to inspire and challenge

is a balanced and objective analysis of the teaching of Jesus, based entirely on the priorities which the gospel writers themselves gave to each subject. I hope that I have not only set out the core of the teaching of Jesus, but also given it the emphasis and balance that he did.

'I confined myself to Matthew, Mark and Luke simply because most of the actual teaching of Jesus is to be found in the first three gospels. Where an insight from John's Gospel helps to illuminate a point in the synoptic accounts, I have not hesitated to introduce it, especially when considering the teaching of Jesus about his own identity and purpose, which are among the great themes of the fourth gospel.'

For ease of reference, the teachings of Jesus are placed in alphabetical order, with the final chapters focusing on Jesus teaching about himself. Key Bible passages are included in full. In the following extract, however, the Bible reference only is given due to the space restraints in this magazine.

Purpose of life

Read Matthew 5:13–16

For the most succinct answer to the question, 'What is the purpose of life?' one would have to turn to John's Gospel. 'This is eternal life, that they may know you, the only true God, and Jesus Christ whom you have sent' (17:3). That is not, of course, the language of the synoptic Gospels, for the most part, yet there is an intriguing exception. It is known to biblical scholars as the 'Johannine thunderbolt', because suddenly, right in the middle of both Matthew's and Luke's Gospels, come these words from the lips of Jesus: 'All things have been handed over to me by my Father; and no one knows the Son except the Father, and no one knows the Father except the Son and anyone to whom the Son chooses to reveal him' (Matthew 11:27; compare Luke 10:22). There is the unmistakable 'style' of the Jesus of the fourth Gospel, claiming that true 'knowledge' of God is only available through 'the Son', and those to whom the Son 'chooses to reveal him'. So in the whole Gospel record there is a unanimous message: to know God is the 'chief end' of humanity, and it is through Jesus Christ alone that he can be fully known. The purpose of life is to know God.

But if that is the great goal, then what are its particulars? For many people, 'knowing God' is an elusive, even nebulous kind of idea. One would expect Jesus the teacher to flesh it out in terms that ordinary people can understand and respond to. And that is, of course, exactly what he does.

Here, in these well-known words, the great goal is expressed in two contrasting particulars. These words are, of course, part of the Sermon on the Mount, which was addressed not to the 'crowds' but to 'his disciples' (see Matthew 5:1). They are the citizens of the new kingdom, the kingdom of God, and Jesus is now setting out for them what life to kingdom standards means. Those who want to 'know God' must, of necessity, be members of that kingdom, or how can they hope to see the king?

And the members of that kingdom are called to be both 'salt' and 'light'—two contrasting roles. Salt, in the ancient world, had two uses. Firstly, and most importantly, it was a preservative. Before the days of refrigeration, salt was the only way to keep meat, for instance, from going bad during the months when it was not naturally available. Salt kept corruption at bay. Salt inhibited the advance of decay.

Secondly, salt (as it does still today) brought the full flavour out of things, turning what was otherwise bland and insipid into a delight for the palate.

The disciples of Jesus, the people of the kingdom, were to fulfil both of those functions in the world. They would hold back by their witness and life the advance of corruption and decay in society. And they would bring flavour and zest into lives which without them would be bland. The kingdom spelt colour, life, hope, imagination, beauty—and they were the 'salt' that would release those gifts of God into the world.

At the same time, they were to be 'light'—indeed, 'the light of the world'. In John's Gospel Jesus calls himself 'the light of the world' (John 8:12), but his followers were called to reflect that divine light into their surroundings. Light shows up what is evil; light dispels darkness; light brings hope and encouragement; light reveals the safe path. In all of those ways the disciples were to be light. It was their calling, an outworking of the great goal of knowing God. They were not to 'know God', in other words, in a selfish, private, little cocoon of piety. They were to know God and represent him, as salt and light, in the world in which he had put them.

When Jesus called his first disciples it was with a rather odd invitation: 'Follow me and I will make you fish for people' (Mark 1:17). I don't think he was saying that their sole calling as his followers was to 'catch' other people and bring them into his kingdom, though that idea is certainly contained in his words. What he was saying, surely, was that if they followed him he would give them new goals, far greater than running a little fishing business on the banks of Galilee. 'Follow me, and I will transform your life … follow me, and nothing will be the same again … follow me, and you will bring light to dark places and the joy of life to those who live empty lives.' Follow me, in other words, and you will 'know God', and share him with others.

TO REFLECT

We all need goals in life, the feeling that it's going somewhere, that it has purpose and meaning. How can this teaching of Jesus help me to set my sights on the 'great goal' and on the particular goals which will make it real for me?

Other passages you may wish to consult:

Matthew 5:48;
Matthew 11:27, 28;
Luke 4:18,19;
Luke 10:20

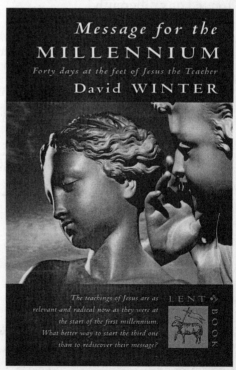

Message for the Millennium is BRF's Lent book for 1999 and is available from your local Christian bookshop or, in case of difficulty, from BRF using the order form on page 159.

Message for the
MILLENNIUM
Forty days at the feet of Jesus the Teacher
David WINTER

The teachings of Jesus are as relevant and radical now as they were at the start of the first millennium. What better way to start the third one than to rediscover their message?

LENT BOOK

The Living Word

Colin Bennetts

The idea of turning to an ancient book for guidance into the 21st century is, on the face of it, very odd. Of course, there are those who revere Old Moore's *Almanac* or the writings of Nostradamus, but in reality they are not taken all that seriously. So why should the book we call the Bible be treated any differently?

The Bible is not one book, of course, but sixty-six books bound together in one volume for convenience. Its diversity is staggering. Written over the course of at least one thousand years by about forty different authors, the idea that it might have a common thread running through it, let alone a coherent message, seems highly improbable. Moreover, the worldview it represents is so alien to our own. It is pre-scientific in virtually every sense of the word: physical, psychological, biological, sociological. Add to that the relatively narrow geographical area it covers, a few Middle Eastern countries and part of the Mediterranean, and you may be left wondering whether it has any relevance to the last century, let alone the next.

And yet, despite all these apparent limitations, the Bible remains the world's best selling book. Countless people have claimed and still do claim that it is one of the most significant ways by which God speaks to them, and as a result of that encounter they find their lives changed for ever. I have to say that I am one of those people, for reasons that I shall try to explain.

First, I find that there is an honesty about the Bible. It's there as we meet Jacob, the one who makes his way in life by manipulating others, David who gives in to sexual temptation, Jonah who finds himself unwillingly caught up in God's

I find that there is an honesty about the Bible

mission. Then there is Thomas whose scepticism excludes him from the community of faith, Saul whose religion breeds a terrible self-righteousness, Peter whose bravado is so easily exchanged for betrayal. The honesty of the Bible lies in its realistic portrayal of very fallible human beings, people whose experiences resonate so loudly with our own.

But alongside this is the glorious fact that not one of them is beyond the rescuing power of God. This rescuing God is described by Bishop John Saxbee as 'the God who loves us just as we are, but who loves us too much to leave us there'. The Bible has an amazing ability to move us from the particular to the universal, to paint sad, ordinary, everyday weaknesses against the timeless background of God's offer of forgiveness and new life. It's this timeless quality that will carry the Bible safely beyond the striking of the millennium clock, because the human condition is not going to change with a new date on the calendar.

The God who holds the mirror up to human society, revealing us for what we are, also reveals *himself* to us through the Bible. But often

As we go to the crib to find the child, so we go to the Scriptures to find the Christ

there is something tantalizing about this revelation; it does not happen all at once. I remember a quiz game from the old days of black and white television. First you were shown a close-up shot of a familiar object, usually taken from an odd angle. If you guessed what it was immediately, you scored full marks, but most competitors needed the camera to pull back a considerable way before they were able to identify the briefcase, record player or stiletto-heeled shoe. The initial shot was not so much 'untrue' as incomplete. I believe it is for that kind of reason that we need to read the Bible as a whole, to grasp the overall sweep of its message. As we do that, we find our attention drawn inescapably to the person of Jesus. It was Martin Luther who said that 'as we go to the crib to find the child, so we go to the Scriptures to find the Christ'. It becomes axiomatic, therefore, that the Bible is not an end in itself, but a means to an end. The written word is that which leads us to the living Word, God's complete and final revelation of his nature and his purposes of love.

It is when we come to understand the purpose of the Bible in this way that we also begin to see the value of regular, daily Bible reading. Far too many Christians find that reading the Bible is a chore. In the end, they either give it up as a bad job or stick with it out of a sense of guilt. If, on the other hand, we see it, quite shamelessly, as a means to an end, as a fruit waiting to be squeezed before it gives up its juice, then we are much more likely to enjoy it. Part of that squeezing will involve us in an interrogation of the text. We shall refuse to go to it just for a few blessed thoughts; rather we shall bombard it with a whole range of basic questions like 'who…?' 'how…?' and specially 'why…?' We will find ourselves giving the text a really hard time until it surrenders its treasures to us. If it is true that we are closer to God when we are struggling with him than when we are ignoring him, so, I believe, that same God expects us to work at our relationship with the Living Word through his written word.

This kind of rigorous, robust study of the Bible is, I believe, vital if we are going to offer a credible account of our faith in the next century. We are not called to invent a new gospel for a new millennium. We are required to wrestle with the eternal truths of the faith, biblical truths which are Christ-centred, and communicate them in a manner which is accessible to the new age. Only those who are bilingual, speaking the language of the Bible and the language of contemporary society, will be equipped for that task.

Rigorous, robust study of the Bible is vital

Colin Bennetts is Bishop of Coventry and Vice-Chariman of the BRF Board of Trustees.

An interview with Brian Ogden

'My late mother was a great hoarder—envelopes, foil containers, coffee jars, and far-flung relations with whom she regularly kept in touch. She was also committed to the local parish church, where she first came into contact with BRF Bible reading notes. She became such an avid reader of the notes that the parish church carried on sending them to her after she left the parish and she continued reading them until her death at the age of ninety. Not being one ever to throw things away, she had a fine collection of BRF notes dating back over many years. Thus I owe my introduction to BRF to my mother, to whom also I owe my allegiance to the Church of England, although I've also enjoyed worshipping in other denominations.'

Brian Ogden has spent most of his life working with children in one capacity or another. After many years as a member of the Church Army, he trained as a primary teacher at Keswick Hall College of Education in Norwich and taught in a number of schools. He also held the role of Advisor in Religious Education both in the diocese of Peterborough and in Chelmsford diocese.

Brian first gained success as a children's writer with his *Maximus Mouse* series of books (published by Scripture Union). To date over fifty thousand copies of these popular stories have been sold. It was whilst leading a workshop on the *Maximus Mouse* stories at a children's Arts Day in Richmond that Brian came into contact with BRF as an established writer. BRF's children's editor, Sue Doggett, was also leading a workshop at the day and invited Brian to contribute to the *Livewires* range of Bible adventures for 8–10s. *Livewires* uses the Bible very much more explicitly than the *Maximus Mouse* stories and Brian found that the experience of writing *Tiptoes and Fingertips* led him to think more widely about the presentation of Bible stories for children of all ages. This encouraged him to look carefully at the different approaches which might be taken to help children learn more about the Bible through the art of storytelling.

'One of the saddest aspects of working with children today is their almost total lack of any biblical foundation. In the past, authors could assume that certain stories and facts were widely known and could be built upon. This is no longer the case and any writer for the children of the next millennium can presume nothing by way of biblical knowledge. Livewires is designed to introduce children to a wide range of Bible stories and characters, some well known, others less so, through a cartoon-style medium, familiar to primary children.'

It was against this background that Brian and Sue started to explore ways to reach younger children and soon *On the Story Mat* started to take shape. The books are set within a recognizable reception classroom. Mrs Jolley, the teacher, uses an incident involving the children to introduce a Bible story. These are today's children, who argue and fight, make friends and fall out with each other. Identification by the reader is an essential ingredient of the stories; not simply identification by behaviour and attitude, but the equally important compatibility of language.

'An experiment I carry out on school visits from time to time is to suggest to the children that something very good has occurred at home. The next day they come to school and share this event with their friends. We then list the words they would use. Only a year or two ago everything was "great" or "fab". But language is evolving, for better or worse, and today you can expect "cool", "ex" (for excellent), and "fantastic". Try it for yourselves.'

January 1998 saw the publication of the first two Story Mat books—*Sometimes the donkey is right* and *Best friends*—with two further titles, *Shepherds and angels* and *Too busy to listen*, coming out in the September of that year.

On the Story Mat is written primarily for five to six year olds, who are gaining confidence in learning to read for themselves. But the books have been used successfully with younger children who enjoy having the stories read to them. The books are delightfully illustrated by Simon Smith, a talented artist who used to be a primary teacher himself and knows exactly how to depict a reception class! Each book contains three Old and four New Testament stories; so in the first six books planned, over forty Bible stories will be introduced to very young children.

With his growing success as a children's author, Brian has worked as a full-time writer and visitor to schools for the past two years. He introduces a lot of humour into his stories, which he puts down to having sat through countless rather tedious assemblies!

'Children appreciate humour and they respond to it. Humour is a vehicle for participating in a story and the story is then more likely to be remembered. Jesus drew children to himself because he understood their needs.'

Brian writes from the point of view of the child and has researched carefully to ensure that the backgrounds, the characters and the experiences of the children in Mrs Jolley's class are real and believable. His books have been widely used both for school and class assemblies and read by children in church and at home, with or without adult involvement. Brian has enjoyed exploring the real world of the reception class as the vehicle to bring the Bible to young children, and has enjoyed seeing it grow from the aspect of his work which was his starting point. This was the deliberate choice of 'talking animal' stories in order to grasp the imagination of the child.

'Children relate to animals in a very positive way. They are not threatened by them, but, at the same time, can fully understand the point of the story. But animals have to be believable—you might have a church mouse, but there is unlikely to be a church elephant!'

In fact, Brian makes his animal stories so believable that a teacher once

told him how a group of children in her class had been found peering through the floorboards in a church they were visiting. When asked what they were doing, they replied that they were looking to see if Maximus Mouse was anywhere in sight!

On average, Brian visits twenty schools per term, speaking to well over three thousand children in that time. He likes to begin the day by taking the school assembly and then spends time in each classroom, discussing story writing and encouraging the children themselves to write.

'I always draw the comparison between the children and myself as authors, with the class teacher in the role as their editor. It comes as a surprise to them to see a manuscript covered in pencil marks by my editor. And they do look a little shocked when I speak of re-drafting a story five, six or seven times.'

Schools often use the opportunity Brian's visits provide to get the children to write letters to him. Occasionally, these will spark off an idea for a new story. Sometimes the letters give very positive feedback of a particular book.

Of *Best friends* Jade wrote:

I really like the story because it makes you think about your friends and it makes you happy. My favourite part is when the teacher hears the two girls talking and

hears the two boys talking.

After one of Brian's visits, Stacey wrote:

After you came to the school I have read a lot of books. I enjoy reading now. I never liked reading before. I think you have encouraged me to read a lot more.

David wrote:

Thank you for coming to school. I really enjoyed your visit. Normally, I don't like writing, but now I'm more confident, I can hardly stop.

And most honest of all—a letter from Luke:

I liked it when you came. I liked it a lot better than Maths, well anything is better than Maths!

All Brian's stories end with a prayer. After one visit to a County school in Stevenage a little girl asked her teacher at the end of the day, 'Could we please say a prayer before we go home?'

In your prayers, please pray for those who write for the children of the millennium, that the new century may be one in which children grow up to know and love the Bible.

Four titles in the range are currently available. See inside back cover for details. All are available from your local Christian bookshop or, in case of difficulty, from BRF using the order form on page 159.

1 and 2 Thessalonians

Over the next two weeks we shall be reading the two letters to the Thessalonians. The first of these was, beyond much doubt, written by Paul; the second quite conceivably not. We shall therefore have to consider questions of authorship with some care in order to be sure of our grounds for interpreting the two letters. We must acknowledge the uncertainty that exists with regard to the second. The first letter also has some critical problems. I begin by setting Paul's relations with the church in Thessalonica in historical relief.

Paul was in Macedonia between September AD48 and April AD50. He divided his time, so it seems, equally between Philippi and Thessalonica. He must have stayed at least a year in each place, given the nature of the travelling conditions. Both churches are greeted by Paul in fond terms in the letters he wrote to them. He seems to have derived a great deal of pleasure from this early period in his ministry. He particularly praises the quality of Christian life in Thessalonica (1 Thessalonians 1:6–8; cf. Philippians 2:14–16).

The relationship between the two Thessalonian letters has prompted disagreement among scholars. Some link them together while others detect as many as four original letters behind the two New Testament texts. The view taken here is that there may be more than one letter behind 1 Thessalonians. There are problems in the flow of material as it stands, and these are best addressed by the theory that the letter has been compiled from more than one of Paul's writings. This process shows the respect in which Paul's letters were held as they began to be collected in the later first century AD.

The authenticity of 2 Thessalonians is more difficult to sustain. If the letter was written by Paul himself, it must have been penned within a reasonably short time of 1 Thessalonians: they both address a similar situation of persecution. But there are also significant differences in language, style and theology between the two letters which make this view hard to accept. The fact that the letter was perhaps not written by Paul does not call into question its value within the canon of New Testament literature. This means that it has an equal inspirational value to 1 Thessalonians for readers today. The practice of forming a canon-within-a-canon, although this is often done by readers of the New Testament, is not to be encouraged if it leads only to a comparison of the relative merits of the pieces of literature concerned. 2 Thessalonians was written, in all probability, by someone who knew and admired Paul and who wanted to adapt Paul's teaching for the needs of a later generation. It entered the New Testament through its presumed connection with Paul. We must read the letter on its terms, not ours, and allow 2 Thessalonians to have its impact on our imagination in the same way as 1 Thessalonians.

4–10 JANUARY   1 THESSALONIANS 1:1—4:12

---

1   In praise of faith   *Read 1 Thessalonians 1:1–10*

1 Thessalonians opens with a characteristic address and salutation which praises the faith of the Thessalonian community and reminds them of what God has done for them. Verse 7 in particular expresses Paul's admiration for his converts in Thessalonica: 'You became an example to all the believers in Macedonia and in Achaia.' It seems that their faith and perseverance were well known throughout the Greek world. This no doubt reflects Paul's careful teaching among them and his efforts over a period in the Thessalonian region.

Paul does not understand this faithfulness, however, as a purely human work. He firmly states in verse 4 that God had chosen the Thessalonians, and the concept of divine election is prominent in this passage. There is an important theological agenda in this statement. In this, almost certainly the earliest of his letters, Paul articulates the conviction that God has chosen the Gentiles. This was the cause of an important controversy in early Christianity which is described more clearly in Galatians 2 and Acts 15. The resolution of this controversy tended towards Paul's position on the *inclusion* of the Gentiles, which he saw as his life's work following his encounter with Jesus on the Damascus road. That explains his positive attitude in this passage towards Gentile Christians.

The most important part of this section of the letter is its conclusion (vv. 9–10). This is widely regarded as a summary of Paul's teaching to Gentiles: 'You turned to God from idols, to serve a living and true God, and to wait for his Son from heaven, whom he raised from the dead—Jesus, who rescues us from the wrath that is coming.' Traditional Jewish polemic against idolatry stands to the fore here. Paul retains this even when writing as a Christian. The passage is an early explanation of why Paul thought it important that the gospel be preached to the Gentiles: it is because the living and true God is the God of the whole world—he has no rival. It must therefore be true, as even some Jewish writers of the period were prepared to recognize, that the Gentiles are included in the offer of eschatological salvation. Accordingly, Paul travelled to Macedonia and preached the gospel there.

The second half of this summary (v. 10) explains the eschatological conviction that inspired early Christianity. ('Eschatology' comes from the Greek *eschaton*, meaning 'last', 'final'. 'Eschatology' refers to Jewish and Christian beliefs about the 'last things', events which were thought to mark the end of the present world order and precede the final coming of God's kingdom on earth.) This was the belief that Jesus, who had been made a divine being in his resurrection from the dead, would return from heaven as Lord and Messiah to preside over the kingdom of God. The thrust of this passage is that Jesus will deliver Christian believers from the final outpouring of God's wrath. The sinners will then be purged from the kingdom and the redeemed will enjoy a new form of life there with their Messiah. We shall discover more about Paul's understanding of eschatology as our reading of the letters proceeds.

2　**The preacher and his family**　*Read 1 Thessalonians 2:1–12*

Paul initially engages in some characteristic defence of his preaching. This is a familiar feature of his letters. We should not think that it springs from personal insecurity or a psychological problem. Verse 2 gives the grounds of this rhetoric: Paul says that he reacts to 'great opposition' which hampered his preaching of the gospel. This opposition was accompanied by physical mistreatment at Philippi, so he says, but the nature of this mistreatment is not specified. It seems, on the basis of verse 3, that Paul may have been accused of preaching from impure motives at Thessalonica. Chapter 2 constitutes his vigorous rebuttal of this criticism. What he preaches does not stem from 'deceit or impure motives or trickery'. It comes direct with the power and authority of God.

In this context Paul includes another familiar protestation. He did not come to the Thessalonians 'with a pretext for greed' (v. 5). The question of money is involved here. It seems from elsewhere in Paul's letters that he earned his own living in the course of his preaching campaigns (cf. 2 Thessalonians 3:8). Paul specifically refutes the implied charge of sponging. Although, as an apostle, he *might* have made demands for financial support (v. 7), in practice he did not do so. He 'worked night and day, so that we might not burden any of you while we proclaimed to you the gospel of God' (v. 9).

This section of the letter gives an important insight into the social position of the itinerant preacher in the ancient world. It seems that some preachers peddled their message for profit. For Paul, as for all preachers of integrity, this raised the question of the authenticity of the message. Those who depend for their support on their preaching face the temptation to adapt their message to suit the needs and interests of the fee-paying audience. Paul will have none of this. His gospel comes direct from God. For this reason Paul thinks himself beholden to behave with a divinely authenticated integrity. His analogy for this is that of the father and children (v. 11), which suits his statement in the later letter, Romans, that Christian people are children of God by adoption (Romans 8:15). This family relationship has been brought into being by the sacrifice of Jesus the Son. Paul thinks it will achieve a permanent and visible status when Jesus the Son returns from heaven (1:10). The relationship between Paul and the Thessalonian Christians is that of family members and not of a client and patrons.

3 Religion and hostility *Read 1 Thessalonians 2:13–20*

This is a difficult section of the letter. The major problem is that Paul here engages in a vitriolic assault on the Jews which no Christian would want to maintain in the aftermath of the Nazi Holocaust of the Second World War.

The way in which this assault is introduced needs careful statement. Paul is not so much criticizing the Jews *prima facie* as comparing the treatment of the Thessalonian Christians by their Gentile compatriots to the way in which Jews had treated the (Jewish) Christians in Palestine. The language is, however, by modern standards, intemperate: '(They) killed both the Lord Jesus and the prophets, and drove us out; they displease God and oppose everyone by hindering us from speaking to the Gentiles so that they may be saved. Thus they have constantly been filling up the measure of their sins; but God's wrath has overtaken them at last' (vv. 15–16).

The background to this statement is the fierce hostility that broke out between zealous Jews and Jewish Christians (even before this name was invented) consequent on the preaching by the latter of the crucified Jesus as Messiah. Zealous Jews took offence at this preaching because of the manner in which Jesus met his death. Crucifixion—which involved the exhibition of a body on a gibbet—infringed the regulation of Deuteronomy 21:23 concerning the display of a mutilated body. That Jesus had been crucified was taken by the zealous Jews as a sign of his rejection by God. It followed that one who was rejected by God could not be the Messiah, the person chosen by God.

The Messiahship of Jesus was an integral part of early Jewish Christian preaching. The guarantee for the Christians that Jesus was Messiah was the strong conviction which broke out almost immediately after his death that God had raised him to new life —specifically, the life of a heavenly being who shared the glory of God. This is what was meant by early Christian belief in the resurrection. This notion that Jesus the executed criminal was the heavenly Lord was, by itself, responsible for the hostility that broke out between the followers of Jesus and Jews of other persuasions. It stands with great vigour behind the present passage.

Paul takes the view, *post Christum*, that the Jews had to commit a specified number of sins before God's wrath would overtake them. This belief is essentially a deterministic one and derives from apocalyptic circles, which emphasized the revelation (Greek *apokalypsis*) of the secrets of God's salvation (examples of apocalyptic writings in the Bible include Daniel 7–12 and Revelation). It is a matter of debate whether 'the wrath of God', as it is used in Paul's theology, is personally mandated by God or merely an impersonal retributive force. There are no grounds for seeing as merely impersonal in this passage, however unpalatable that conclusion may be. Paul looks forward to the time when God will punish the Jews for their sins as one of the events of the eschatological climax. The best we can say is that the polarized distinction between judgment and salvation is a recognized feature of apocalyptic thought and that many, if not most, professional theologians would want to phrase things more cautiously today. It is perfectly certain that Christians must respect Jews and acknowledge the integrity of their religion.

4 Confidence and anxiety *Read 1 Thessalonians 3:1–5*

Paul continues in more positive vein. The point of his assault against those who hinder the gospel is his insistence that the gospel as such cannot be hindered. It comes with the power of God, which human beings cannot resist. Paul's over-arching message is that 'no one (will) be shaken by these persecutions' (v. 3). The further apocalyptic device of prognostication comes to his aid in this respect. Paul says that he had told the Thessalonians about persecution beforehand. Apocalyptic literature often sets limits to a projected crisis to help its readers survive and overcome it. Paul appears to be doing something similar here.

This does not mean, on his own admission, that Paul was entirely confident the Thessalonians would survive the experience of conflict. Something of the real Paul shines through verse 5: 'When I could bear it no longer, I sent (Timothy) to find out about your faith; I was afraid that somehow the tempter had tempted you and that our labour had been in vain.' Not even apocalyptic language is a guarantee that people will do what Paul wants them to! Perpetuating the father–children analogy, Paul feels a natural anxiety for his churches which surfaces in his desire to discern that all is well.

5 Faith and prayer, love and holiness
Read 1 Thessalonians 3:6–13

Timothy's mission produces reassuring news. All is well despite the intervening trouble. This leads Paul to rejoice about the state of the community's faith (v. 7). Such a reference can easily sound forced to modern ears. We must remember, however, that all early Christian references to 'faith' always mean 'faith *in something*' and never 'simple trust' in the abstract. In this case, 'faith' means 'faith in God', which has been made possible by the death and resurrection of Jesus. Such faith distinguished the Christians from others in their social world and frequently led to misunderstanding of the Christians because of the manner of the death of Jesus. This is by no means a trite reference but in every sense a practical one.

The concomitant of faith is prayer (v. 10). Paul prays that whatever is lacking in their faith will be restored and that he will soon see the Thessalonians face to face. The passage ends with a benediction which, on the theory presented in these notes, was originally the benediction for the earlier of the two letters which now comprise 1 Thessalonians. The benediction reveals something of the self-understanding of the early Christian community. The call for mutual love (v. 12) has the social function of erecting barriers against outsiders and it reinforces readers in their sense of corporate solidarity. This is bound up with the concept of 'holiness' which is introduced in verse 13. 'Holiness' is the very character of God himself, shared to a lesser degree by the angels. The call for holiness reminds the community to see themselves as an outpost of heaven on earth in which perceptibly different standards must distinguish them from their pagan environment. The adjective 'blameless' in the last verse of chapter 3 has a double edge. It is both a call to ethical seriousness and a tacit reminder that absolute integrity in the face of eschatological judgment can be provided by God alone. Holiness will be *provided* by God so that God's strict standards are appropriately met. This is the doctrine of justification.

6 What God does and what believers do
Read 1 Thessalonians 4:1–12

Paul continues with ethical instruction. The word 'Finally' at the beginning of chapter 4 is a further indication that more than one letter is fused together here. What follows is authentically Pauline but we must remember the combination of sources.

The goal of ethical action, as Paul defines it, is 'to please God' (v. 1). As I said earlier, there is more than one edge to this understanding of ethics. The key to Paul's understanding is the term 'sanctification', which he uses in verse 3. 'Sanctification' recognizes that the process of salvation will not be complete until Christians pass through the eschatological judgment consequent upon the return of Jesus. It is thus a progressive process, although Paul believes that the decisive change has been achieved already with the death and resurrection of Jesus. Sanctification is what God does to the Christian believer. The Christian believer must respond by allowing the process to take place in his or her life.

This ethical instruction demands a clear separation from the standards of the surrounding pagan world: 'Not... like the Gentiles, who do not know God' (v. 5) is the refrain of this section. This is doubtless based on traditional Jewish horror of Gentile practices, but something more than Jewish hostility is implied. The point is that Christians must abstain from such activity on account of their *Christian* calling.

An important theme of the Thessalonian correspondence is introduced by verse 11, where Paul urges readers to 'work with your hands'. It seems that some in the community had been so far attracted by Paul's preaching that the return of Jesus from heaven was near that they had given up their jobs in expectation of the imminent end. This is an issue that will cause particular concern in 2 Thessalonians. Paul introduces the matter almost obliquely. It prepares the way for his earliest eschatological teaching, which follows in the next section.

Apocalyptic language, although relatively often encountered in the New Testament, is a difficult complex of thought for readers today to understand. Although we can understand as an idea what it might mean for God to predetermine human events, this in fact raises complex philosophical issues about divine providence and human free will which must not be circumvented by modern interpreters. The final answer is no doubt that, although God knows the choices we will make, he cannot be said to determine them himself—still less to make our wrong and sinful choices for us! Paul's all too human anxiety about the well-being of his churches is a necessary reminder of the part that we must play in shaping the world according to our faith, even when the issue of hopeful trust in God is a matter of critical concern. We cannot rely on God to 'do it all' for us.

11–17 JANUARY   1 THESSALONIANS 4:13— 2 THESSALONIANS 3:18

1 Hope and meaning *Read 1 Thessalonians 4:13–18*

There is a strong sense in which eschatology undergirded the whole of the early Christian movement. Judaism, particularly in its apocalyptic literature, had produced a variety of eschatological belief in which the hope for the Messiah often assumed a central role. Christianity came to birth in the experience of hopefulness that was the resurrection of Jesus. The distinctive feature of Christian eschatology was the belief that the last things had *already* been inaugurated with the resurrection of Jesus, and that they would be brought to completion with the return of Jesus from heaven.

The issue that undergirds this passage is the question of whether natural human death before the return of Jesus meant that those who had died would miss out on the eschatological benefits. Paul replies that this is emphatically not the case.

Christians are not to grieve as those without hope (v. 13), because God will raise even the dead at the return of Jesus (v. 14). This is the event described in 4:16: 'For the Lord himself, with a cry of command, and with the archangel's call and with the sound of God's trumpet, will descend from heaven, and the dead in Christ will rise first.' Those who are still alive, among whose number Paul evidently reckons himself, will be caught up into the clouds to greet the Lord, apparently to escort him back to earth (v. 17). This teaching is to be a source of great encouragement in the Christian community (v. 18).

Part of the challenge of Christian theology today is to wrestle with such ancient texts, whose world-view is no longer the same as ours, and to find meaning in literature whose outlook and hopes are frankly dated. Many, perhaps most, Christians today do not think that Jesus will return from heaven, but this does not mean that eschatology is removed from the Christian agenda. It means by contrast that the nature of Christian eschatology must be the subject of careful reinterpretation. We still enjoy the hope of an encounter with our Lord, even if this is likely to be through the processes of death and not as an encounter with a supernatural being on earth (cf. Philippians 1:21ff).

No reader of the New Testament can set aside the challenge of interpretation. It will not do to pretend that Christian belief today is precisely the same as in the New Testament period. We must acknowledge the differences in culture and outlook and make an appropriate judgment on that basis. But this is not the same as saying that the relevance of the New Testament literature is superseded. The difference between the two views must be duly acknowledged.

2 Falling into sleep   *Read 1 Thessalonians 5:1–11*

Eschatological teaching is accompanied by ethical exhortation. Paul reiterates the teaching of Jesus that 'the day of the Lord will come like a thief in the night' (v. 2). This is one of the relatively few places in Paul's writings where he makes clear allusion to the words of Jesus. The point is that those who find security around them will suddenly be overtaken by calamity. This is the calamity of the judgment inaugurated by the returning Jesus.

The real point of the passage for interpreters today is the way in which the eschatology undergirds the ethical exhortation. The early Christians did not know when Jesus would return. We do not know when we will die. The eschatological conditions are to this extent the same across the centuries. The basis of Christian eschatology is the uncertainty of our knowledge of the eschatological future, combined with the central place that eschatology occupies in Christian theology. There is a considerable force for contemporary Christian readers in the statement of verse 8: 'Since we belong to the day, let us be sober, and put on the breastplate of faith and love, and for a helmet the hope of salvation.'

The characteristic word of this section is 'sleep'. Paul uses 'sleep' as a metaphor for the failure to maintain vigilance in the last days. The implication is that those who sleep will miss the returning Lord and that they will therefore be liable to eschatological judgment. One can only presume that the reason this message is brought so strongly to the fore in this text is that people needed reminding of ethical teaching, and that some did indeed 'fall away' from the primitive Christian communities.

3 Closing exhortations   *Read 1 Thessalonians 5:12–28*

The letter ends with further exhortation which matches the tone that we observed at the beginning of chapter 4. Here, we gain a practical insight into the problems that beset the Thessalonian community. It seems from verse 12 that people may have been tempted to despise their leaders, probably because there was an evident uncertainty about the nature of Christian eschatological hope in Thessalonica. Verse 14 mentions 'idlers' once again, confirming that this was a substantial problem in Thessalonica. We shall see that 2 Thessalonians relates this to the eschatological controversy, although it is fair to say that, if 2 Thessalonians is not genuinely by Paul, we cannot be certain that the situation addressed by the two letters is the same one.

The short spiritual maxims with which the letter closes are no throw-away conclusion but amongst the most powerful parts of the letter. They are effective because they are easily memorable: 'Rejoice always, pray without ceasing, give thanks in all circumstances; for this is the will of God in Christ Jesus for you' (vv. 16–18).

Among these short one-liners, one in particular seems difficult to understand today: 'Do not despise the words of prophets' (v. 20). 'Prophets' have a bad reputation today. We identify them with astrologers and charlatans and see here a popular phenomenon which has little front-rank relevance to the needs of society. Things could not have been more different in early Christian churches. Prophets were people who spoke the divine will directly to the Christian congregations. They were a recognized class in Christian antiquity, held in rank second only to the apostles (1 Corinthians 12:28) and functioning as important figures of authority. The reference here is again to the message which the prophets brought.

In the light of this criticism of leaders and prophets, we are brought once again to the teaching about eschatology in 4:13–18 as the central part of the letter. This subject will be addressed again in 2 Thessalonians.

4 Active suffering *Read 2 Thessalonians 1:1–12*

Paul—despite the uncertainty over authorship, I shall refer to the author of this letter as Paul—again starts off in boasting mode. He tells the readers that he boasted of their faith and love among the churches of God. This perpetuates the note of affection between the Thessalonians and Paul which 1 Thessalonians had established, and it again brings to the fore the theme of suffering (v. 4).

This theme, like others, needs careful explanation today. One can easily detect a note almost of paranoia in the New Testament literature with its frequent references to crosses and persecutions. Jesus himself is recorded as telling his followers to 'take up' their crosses if they want to follow him. This in part reflects the social situation of the early Christians as people who were misunderstood in the ancient world because of the manner of their leader's death. It also suggests a certain attitude towards the world which was caused by the rejection of pagan ideology and by the belief that the kingdom of God was soon to be established on earth.

Persecution and violence have been important themes in Christian theology down the ages. A particularly important response was articulated by Dietrich Bonhoeffer, who perished at the hands of the Nazis during the Second World War. Bonhoeffer criticized the tradition of 'passive resistance', by which he meant the resigned acceptance of suffering. Such passive resistance was a feature of some Jewish groups in their attitude towards Rome during the period when the New Testament documents were written. Bonhoeffer argued that truly Christian suffering must have an active face in the sense that it sets out to resist the forces of evil.

The second half of 2 Thessalonians 1 can hardly be said to describe 'passive resistance'. Paul is uncompromising in his view of eschatological retribution: 'It is indeed just of God to repay with affliction those who afflict you' (2 Thessalonians 1:6). He goes on to say that the Lord Jesus will 'inflict vengeance' on those who do not know God and refuse to obey the gospel. The point here is not so much that Paul is gloating in the knowledge that these people will be punished but that he anticipates the final triumph of good over evil. He encourages the churches in their faith and love while this vision of the new age goes through its birth pangs.

This is powerful literature indeed. Christians who engage with it must ask themselves how they view the injustices of the world in which they live. They must also strive to gain a clear theological articulation of why such injustices must be challenged in the name of Christ. A *reasoned understanding* of what is to be done is at the heart of any action of this kind. We must not only act but also understand the reasons for our course of action. Engagement with 2 Thessalonians 1 helps to resource critical thinking of this kind.

5   A time of restraint   *Read 2 Thessalonians 2:1–16*

Paul now presents further eschatological teaching. There is a difference in tone between this passage and 1 Thessalonians 4. There, Paul writes against the background of an imminent eschatology in which he thinks that he will be alive to witness the return of the Lord from heaven. The scheme here is more elaborate and seems set against the opinions of those who think the Lord's return will happen imminently. I find this a significant difference in outlook.

The difference in tone is obvious from the outset: 'We beg you, brothers and sisters, not to be quickly shaken in mind or alarmed' (vv. 1–2). A letter purporting to be by Paul had apparently been written in which it was claimed that the 'day of the Lord' had arrived already (v. 2). 2 Thessalonians is therefore set against the view that the kingdom of God is a present reality. Paul reinforces this point by the scheme of eschatology that he introduces. In order to demonstrate the implausibility of supposing that the kingdom was already present, he says that certain events have yet to happen. He anticipates the appearance of a specific figure called 'the lawless one' (v. 3) and says that this person will even take his seat in the temple of God, 'declaring himself to be God' (v. 4). Paul draws here on the symbolism of the book of Daniel and perhaps also on the memory of Caligula's invasion of the temple in AD39. There are parallels also with the 'antichrist' language that is used in the Johannine epistles.

Verse 6 sets the tenor of the passage. The view that the kingdom of God is present is an illusion. The seemingly peaceful nature of the present indicates only that the lawless one is restrained. This implies that there is to be a significant increase in hostilities in the future. But, for all this, the outcome of the contest is not left in doubt. The Lord Jesus will destroy the lawless one with the breath of his mouth (v. 8). *That* will be the time when the kingdom is fully here.

Eschatological passages such as these (and thus of course the book of Revelation!) are among the most difficult aspects of the New Testament literature to understand. The sequence of thought in this passage is perhaps as clear as the contemporary meaning of the passage is obscure. Paul offers a scheme of eschatology to counter the view that the promised hopes have been realized already. We should not take this material as a literal prediction of our eschatological future. It does, however, caution us against too enthusiastic a Christianity which makes light of the difficulties (and opportunities) that lie ahead. These must be met with the confidence and courage of faith—and perhaps also with the comforting recognition that not even the great apostle to the Gentiles knew the entirety of what was to come!

6 Closing exhortations, and a warning to the idle
Read 2 Thessalonians 3:1–18

The letter ends, like 1 Thessalonians, with ethical exhortation. Here we have a further, and more powerful, reference to idle people (vv. 6–13). It seems that some had given up their jobs under the belief that the kingdom of God was either imminent or present. Paul's eschatological caution in chapter 2 is the basis for what he says in chapter 3. The author copies what Paul had said in the earlier letter: 'We did not eat anyone's bread without paying for it' (v. 8; cf. 1 Thessalonians 1:9). This leads to the command that those who are idle must return to earning their own living (v. 12).

This is not simply a capitalist work ethic but a real recognition of the place of Christians in society in the late first century. We do not know the identity of these idle ones but presumably they were sufficiently well off to be able to support their idleness from their own means, and were thus perhaps the better-placed in the Thessalonian Christian community. Paul's admonition is set against the charge, documented in other literature, that Christians were social outcasts who threatened the corporate well-being. He tells the Thessalonians by implication not to hold hostages to fortune but to live their lives honourably and peaceably in expectation of what was to come.

In verses 14–15 we have a further indication of the 'exclusive' nature of the early Christian communities. Those who refuse to heed the contents of the letter must be spurned until they adhere to the truth of what is said here. One is reminded of the notorious incident in 1 Corinthians (5:5) where Paul tells his readers to 'hand over' an evil-doer to Satan for the destruction of his flesh in order that he may finally enjoy eschatological salvation. The Christian communities had high standards of separation from outsiders which expressed themselves in one way in ethical activity. Ethics and self-definition are closely associated in early Christian literature.

GUIDELINES

Throughout these two letters, there has been a link between eschatology and ethics. This is a consistent feature of New Testament literature, and it is amongst the hardest of biblical concepts for modern Christianity to utilize. We rightly reinterpret the eschatology of the New Testament, but this does not mean that the ethical call should be any less urgent. Careful consideration must be given to the statement of New Testament ethics today so that the meaning of the material is not lost in the necessary processes of interpretation. This is part of the challenge that faces all readers of the biblical literature.

Further reading

Jerome Murphy-O'Connor, *Paul: A Critical Life*, 1996, sets Paul's writings in the context of his life and ministry.

Karl P. Donfried and I. Howard Marshall, *The Theology of the Shorter Pauline Letters*, Cambridge 1993, contains an accessible discussion of the themes of these letters.

Recent commentaries include those by F.F. Bruce (Word, 1982) and I.H. Marshall (New Century Bible, 1984).

Isaiah 1—39

Isaiah is almost the longest book in the Bible. It is also a book of great themes, teaching us about God and his people. Fortunately, the presence of a number of clear divisions within it makes it manageable to read. Parts of Isaiah 1–39 come from the prophet Isaiah (mentioned in 1:1 and 2:1) who prophesied in Jerusalem during the reigns of the Judean kings Uzziah, Jotham, Ahaz and Hezekiah. So we call him 'Isaiah of Jerusalem', and the references to these kings enables us to date his ministry in the eighth century BC. In parts of these chapters we read threats of God's judgment, even that there would be exile. And for the people of Judah and Jerusalem there was exile in Babylon from 586 to about 536BC.

When we turn to Isaiah 40 we are in a different world, in a time towards the end of the exile. The talk is about return home, and about this being made possible through the policies of the Persian king Cyrus, who had conquered Babylon in 536BC. Then chapters 56–66 seem to come from an even later time, when people are back in their homeland, working—often struggling—to re-establish religious and political life.

There is much material in Isaiah 1–39 that comes from the preaching of the prophet Isaiah of Jerusalem, but there is also material coming from later times. Parts of chapters 13–23, a series of passages about other nations (Oracles against the Nations), come from times later than Isaiah. Chapters 24–27 have a forward look, speaking about the completion of God's purposes on earth. They probably come from various times after the exile. Then chapter 35 is much more like chapters 40–55 than 1–39. Chapters 36–39 are different again, being nearly the same as 2 Kings 18–20 and in the style of the books of Kings.

Yet these various parts have much in common. They all speak about the great and mighty Lord who has plans and purposes for his people. This Lord is holy and righteous, calling his people to look to him for help and strength, and to act towards one another with care and in justice. He calls prophets and others to be his servants. This God is still our God, and to these words of his prophets we now turn.

These notes are based on the New Revised Standard Version.

18–24 JANUARY   **ISAIAH 1:1—5:23**

---

1 Rebellious people *Read Isaiah 1:1–9*

God, his prophet, and his people are the themes of these opening verses of the long book of Isaiah. In verse 1 we are introduced to the prophet, a man called and inspired by God to proclaim his word to his people at a particular historical moment. Then (vv. 2–3) we are to imagine that we are in court: God is the plaintiff, his people the defendants, heaven and earth (no less!) the witnesses. God's complaint is that his people have failed in their relationship with him. They have behaved like rebellious children. In fact they have behaved worse than the animals—at least animals know who is master and acknowledge who is the giver!

Verse 4 has further details about these failures: the people have despised 'the Holy One of Israel', a title for God that is particularly associated with the book of Isaiah. It emphasizes two aspects of God: first that he is 'holy', that is, different from us, supreme over all things, the true subject of our awe and devotion. Yet, second, he has committed himself to a particular people—he is the Holy One *of Israel*. This is the God who must castigate his people, but who still remains committed to them!

Verses 7–9 speak of the parlous situation in which Israel finds herself. The historical background seems to be 701BC when Assyria had conquered much of Judah, leaving only Jerusalem intact. The prophet says that without God's commitment things would have been even worse, the land becoming like the notorious Sodom and Gomorrah, cities that for the Bible represent the depths of human depravity (Genesis 19:24–29). There indeed, 'but for the grace of God', would Jerusalem have gone!

2 Worship, true and false *Read Isaiah 1:10–20*

This is about worship of God—what it is not and what it should be. We should not think of the actual people of Sodom and Gomorrah being addressed here, but that Judah and Jerusalem are *like* Sodom and Gomorrah. That message cannot have made the prophet very popular!

We could read this as a general condemnation of sacrificial worship, and sometimes this and other passages in the Old Testament (for example, Amos 5:21–24) are understood in that way. But the bringing of offerings to God, who has given so much, cannot itself be bad. More likely, what the prophets condemned was not the institution itself, but its abuse. They condemned people who in their daily lives failed to live out the things of God, but who were there at worship with their elaborate sacrifices. Such worship is pointless (v. 13); to God it is distasteful (v. 14). Their prayer is also a mockery—people stretch out their hands expecting to receive, but all they do is to show to God the bloodstains!

There is a way out of this situation: there is hope. People may change their lives (v. 16) and live differently (v. 17). For the Old Testament, seeking justice is more than seeking to get the correct legal ruling: it means behaving uprightly in the world. The practical outworking of that will take place especially among those who are on the margins of society, who are weak and powerless and who need the protection of the strong. In an ancient society, it was the widows and orphans who were particularly vulnerable. Our reading of this passage today should make us prayerfully consider who are today's oppressed people, and what practical steps the Christian Church might take so that its worship is true and spiritual.

The passage ends with a dramatic appeal to these people. The ways of life and death lie before them, as they lie before us all.

3 Jerusalem, sinful yet cleansed *Read Isaiah 1:21–28 and 4:2–6*

Isaiah 1:21–23 presents a sad picture of Jerusalem, no longer 'the faithful city'. Where once there was faithfulness, now there is harlotry (v. 21), and what was once pure now has much impurity within it (v. 22). Verse 23 suggests that both leaders ('princes') and people must share in the blame for this dreadful state of affairs. The historical situation could be the rather sad days of King Ahaz (735–715BC)—a king who in the Old Testament gets a poor 'press'. This is a crisis due not to an invasion of a foreign power, but to corruption within the nation.

Thus the wrath of the Lord will fall upon this city (vv. 24–25). We should not think of God coming in any meaninglessly destructive way. His righteous indignation burns, but it is a wrath that purifies his people—removing the dross, purifying the metal (v. 25). After that has taken place, there will be restoration of the leaders (v. 26). The title 'judges' indicates those who have the responsibility of ruling God's people. The 'counsellors' are those who know how to make sound judgments. When there are good leaders, there will be a renewed city (vv. 27–28).

The renewed city is portrayed in Isaiah 4:2–6, verses which probably do not come from the prophet Isaiah. However, what is important is that an editor has put these passages together in the finished work, and by doing so has spoken truly and profoundly both about God's judgment upon evil, and his ongoing purposes for his people. God's purposes cannot be defeated, even when his people fail to live up to what he has called them to be. Moreover, he is the God who can bring new out of old, making 'beautiful and glorious' (4:2) what was terrible. And for our own age, while we may despair of the life of so many cities and nations, surely God never despairs. Through these Scriptures he continues to show us that he always wills life and righteousness for the cities and nations.

4 The glory of Jerusalem   *Read Isaiah 2:1–5*

This is one of the best-known passages from the book of Isaiah, expressing the confident expectation that in a unity focused on the hill of Zion in Jerusalem, all the nations will find peace. So they will be able to convert their weapons of war into agricultural implements. This is a passage frequently used on Remembrance Sunday, expressing deep longings for peace and for the beneficial use of our resources and technology.

The passage probably does not come from Isaiah. There is much in Isaiah 1–39 that comes from times later than the eighth century BC, and this is one such passage. Its universal tone, its emphasis on all the nations coming to learn the ways and walk in the paths of the Lord God of Israel, seems to reflect a time after the exile in Babylon, an approach found in parts of Isaiah 40–55. The passage also occurs in Micah 4:1–4: perhaps it comes originally from neither Isaiah nor Micah, but it was felt that it would be good to have it in both collections of prophecies. But while there is an emphasis on the universal nature of the call of God (it is to 'many peoples', v. 3), there is no 'missionary' talk. Here are people who will come to walk in God's ways, but we are not told about any Israelite people who might go to them with the 'message'.

Verse 5 is addressed to the people of Israel as they await the glorious fulfilment of what has been spoken about in the previous verses. And so it should speak to us. We long for the days when the kingly reign of the Lord God is accepted throughout the nations, but that must begin *now* with the present community of faith—let us indeed seek to walk in the light of the Lord (v. 5).

The remarkable vision that this prophecy gives us is of the glory of God. It points to the God who is Lord of all nations. His is the glory. The passage is addressed to the peoples of Judah and Jerusalem (people of town and country): let them be ready for the Lord God to do great things; he is not only their God, but he is by right the Lord of all peoples.

5 The vineyard   *Read Isaiah 5:1–7*

Here is one of the Old Testament's parables: the life of the people of Israel is set alongside the life of a vineyard. But the style of the parable is that of a song. The singer must be the prophet, who describes the Lord of the vineyard (God) as his 'beloved'. It is as if the prophet is a close friend of the Lord, rather like a 'best man'. As we read about this vineyard we are intended to understand that it is about Israel—and ourselves!

It says that God has done everything possible for people to ensure their welfare, so that they will yield a 'harvest' for him.

That is the significance of all the detail about the careful preparation of the vineyard—its siting in fertile ground, the vat dug to take the wine, and so on. Little was left to chance!

In verses 3 and 4 the inhabitants of Judah and Jerusalem are invited to cast their verdict as to who is in the wrong, the Lord or the vineyard. There was only one possible answer: the Lord has done everything possible, so the vineyard must be at fault.

Verses 5 and 6 utter words of condemnation upon the vineyard. It is to be closed down, and laid waste. The Lord is pictured as destroying it. Normally, an unproductive vineyard would be abandoned by the vine grower. But the thought of the parable is progressing, and no longer is the talk about an imaginary vineyard, but now about the people of Israel and Judah. This becomes clear in verse 7. It is like the moment of climax in Nathan's parable in 2 Samuel 12, when the prophet turns upon David: 'You are the man!' (v. 7)

All this may seem a harsh word of judgment, but it reminds us that along with privilege goes responsibility. God loves us indeed, but he is the righteous God who calls his people to live righteously. God must burn with holy anger when he sees unrighteousness in the world now. Still today:

He expected justice,
but saw bloodshed;
righteousness,
but heard a cry (v. 7).

6   We are doomed!   *Read Isaiah 5:8–23*

At the beginning of Isaiah 5:8, 11, 18, 20, 21 and 22, NRSV has the word 'Ah'. Other translations have 'Woe'. GNB has 'You are doomed', which does convey the meaning of the original. The prophet is announcing that because of some serious sin, doom is coming upon the people concerned. But it is a series of sins that is spoken of in this passage.

The sin in verses 8–10 is greed on the part of powerful landowning people. This is what may be seen when free market forces are left to operate unhindered, especially if the powerful think only of themselves and do not have regard for the rights of the weak. But the Lord is on the side of the weak (Luke 1:51–53), and he hears their cry (Exodus 3:7). Isaiah proclaimed that the greed of powerful and unscrupulous people would result in their ruin and destruction (vv. 9–10). They were doomed!

In verses 11 and 12 the issue is the luxury and pleasure enjoyed by the wealthy. The privileged people have wealth and leisure to eat and drink all day long; at the same time others are dying of starvation. The holy and righteous God cannot tolerate such behaviour—so a further sentence of 'doom'.

The sequence of 'dooms' is interrupted in verses 13–17 to give some details of the judgment coming upon these sinful people. In historical terms it is a going into exile (v. 13), and we should understand these verses as coming from a time after the beginning of the exile, giving a reason why it took place. 'Sheol' (v. 14) is the place where, for the Old Testament writers, the dead go. It is neither hell nor purgatory, but simply a cold and dark place. It would be much later that a positive belief about death would emerge (Daniel 12:2; John 11:25).

Verses 18 and 19 deal with wrongdoings on the part of powerful and arrogant people. They have become caught up in evil ways, which will in fact destroy them. The depth of sin spoken of in verse 20 describes a person so immersed in wrongdoing that it has become their natural way of life. A reversal of values has taken place. Doom again! So also for those whose pride is in themselves (v. 21), and those so taken up with their drinking that they neglect their responsibilities in society (vv. 22–23).

Some will feel that this is a depressing passage, but will surely acknowledge that the life of our own society today is also depressing. We must read on into the Isaiah book, and elsewhere in our Bibles, to hear how we and our society may be redeemed and remade, but the message of today's scripture is that we are all under the judgment of God, all equally in need of his mercy and love.

Much of what we have read in Isaiah this week will seem to be harsh and judgmental about the lives of people. Other aspects of the matter will be given to us as we read on, but we should avoid the temptation of going straight to the hopeful and comforting parts of the scriptures. We must face up to the parts of the Bible that challenge us about our sins. We have read how God's people of old failed him, and no doubt we are little better today. We too must hear the challenging words of the prophets, so that we may be open to God's renewing and redeeming work within us as individuals, in his Church, and in his world.

A prayer from Private Devotions of 1560

Cleanse me, O God, by the bright fountain of thy mercy, and water me with the dew of thine abundant grace, that, being purified from my sins, I may grow up in good works, truly serving thee in holiness and righteousness all the days of my life.

25–31 JANUARY   **ISAIAH 6:1—12:6**

1   Vision and call   *Read Isaiah 6:1–13*

This is perhaps the best-known chapter of Isaiah, and rightly so, for it deals with most important subjects. The first subject is in verses 1–5: a remarkable vision of the mighty and glorious Lord of all. It seems most likely that this vision was experienced in the temple at Jerusalem. So powerful was the experience that the prophet remembered the year in which it took place (v. 1). But then, perhaps the year of King Uzziah's death was a memorable year: that king had reigned a long time, and the coming years were to turn out to be troubled ones. In time to come, the prophet looked back and saw that that year represented the end of an era. But above all the turmoil of earth there reigns the mighty Lord, and so great is he that the hem of his robe is enough to fill the temple!

Moreover, the Lord is attended by heavenly beings who continually sing his praises (v. 3). 'Holiness' is about God's uniqueness, power, majesty. 'Glory' is that aspect of God's otherness that may be sensed, experienced by a human being. This great God makes his presence felt throughout the earth and when we sense that divine presence, we experience this 'glory'.

Then (the second subject), after having become convicted and cleansed of his sin, the prophet is called to service. And it is an apparently strange commission that is entrusted to him. It seems that he must harden hearts against God, rather than make them open to his will! But then, perhaps this account has been written up in the light of experience. And perhaps things for these people must get worse before they get better. Only as things get really bad will people turn in any deep and meaningful way to the Lord of Hosts. Then there will be hope—great and massive hope—in the remaining remnant of God's people, that is, in the small group of people who are faithful in belief and in God's service.

2 King and prophet   Read Isaiah 7:1–16

War! The little state of Judah is attacked by a coalition of two states, Israel and Syria. In picturesque language (v. 2) we are told how a state of general panic ensues in Jerusalem. So it is that Isaiah the prophet is called to speak a word from God to the king, who was probably inspecting the city water supply in preparation for the coming siege (v. 3). But the prophet is to take with him his son (v. 3) whose name means 'A Remnant will Return', and no doubt there was a message in that name for the king and his people that day. There may not have been much faith in the Lord in evidence on that day, but a day would come when a small group would come back to God in faith.

The main burden of the prophet's message from his God to the king is in the second part of verse 9, and is a ringing call to have faith in God. This does not necessarily mean that the king need take no active preparations for war! But it does perhaps mean that such actions must be undergirded by faith in God.

There needs to be both faith in God and human action.

And then comes the prophet's word about another child—the sign of Immanuel (v. 4). Christians understand that this prophecy has been fulfilled in the life and the work of Jesus Christ—and that is certainly how Matthew understood it (Matthew 1:23). But it seems clear that the prophet was also thinking of something that would happen much sooner than eight centuries into the future. Perhaps he was also saying, quite simply, that a day would come when a woman would give birth to a child and would name the child in celebration of the fact that the threatening danger had now passed away, and that once again God's people had been delivered. But that is not to ignore or deny the fact that, some eight centuries later, God's people would experience an even more wonderful and astounding deliverance in Jesus!

3 The new king   *Read Isaiah 9:2–7*

King Ahaz was a poor king—that is what Isaiah thought. And the books of Kings hardly think any better of him (2 Kings 16). But now the prophet shares a wonderful vision of the day when a much better, even perfect, king would come. And whereas, in the days of Ahaz, because Ahaz was such a poor king, the people would inevitably be in a state of darkness, with this new and great king their situation will be totally transformed (v. 2). Now there will be no more war, for this will be a peaceable kingdom. Yet it will not be peaceable merely through the absence of threats and enemies, but rather because there is a mighty one under whom the people live. Although the birth of this child is portrayed as fairly normal, he is far from being any average or normal person (v. 7)! Four unique titles are given to him, each of them expressed by two words. 'Wonderful Counsellor': literally 'wonder of a counsellor' (the AV was not correct in separating the two words with a comma—and Handel, with the wonderful chorus in *Messiah*, compounded the mistake!) The meaning is that this person is supremely wise, always giving the correct advice. The second title is even more startling—'Mighty God'. Nowhere else in the Old Testament is a king spoken of in such an exalted way. In the Old Testament, kings are very much on the human side of things. But this one is on the Godward side of the equation. The title 'Everlasting Father' speaks about this king being a father and guide to his people for ever. The final title, 'Prince of Peace', refers to the fact that he will bring about conditions in which there will be a real sense of harmony and wholeness, which is something much more than the mere absence of strife and war.

Two things need to be said in response to the question, 'Whom is the prophet speaking about here?' In all probability the prophet did not have any particular historical king in mind, but rather he was saying something about an ideal king. This is a vision of what it might be like one day. And that leads to the second thing: Christians believe that this remarkable prophecy was fulfilled when Jesus was born. It is with very good reason that we so often read this passage at our Christmas carol services. Let us rejoice not only that the promised one has been given to us as individuals, but also that he brings to the whole world his own 'endless peace'.

4 Assyria, called to serve God   *Read Isaiah 10:5–19*

After reading three well-known passages from Isaiah, we turn to one less widely known. It is about the way God works in the world, in particular about the ways in which he works through human beings, sometimes those with great power and authority and at other times those who live very quiet and humble lives. This passage is concerned with the fact that God worked at one stage in the history of the world through the king of Assyria. At a later stage in the book of Isaiah there will be talk about God working through the Persian king, Cyrus (Isaiah 44:28—45:4). We may also ask ourselves whether it was in the purposes of God that the institutions of the Roman Empire made possible the rapid spread of Christianity. Without the peace and the good roads and the common languages, how would it have been possible for the new faith to have been proclaimed so speedily?

Certainly the Old Testament prophets believed that God did work through foreign rulers, and Isaiah speaks of the work that

God accomplishes through the Assyrian king. But something has gone wrong—as it frequently does when people are called to do great works for God. The servants forget that they are servants, and become proud and arrogant. This is what has happened with the king of Assyria. His successes have 'gone to his head' (vv. 8–9), so that now he begins to think that nothing is impossible for him to accomplish (vv. 10–11). As a result of this unpardonable pride the judgment of the Lord must fall upon the Assyrian (vv. 12–14 and 16–19). Let each of us have the humility and grace to ask ourselves:

> *Shall the axe vaunt itself over the one who wields it,*
> *or the saw magnify itself against the one who handles it?*
> *As if a rod should raise the one who lifts it up,*
> *or as if a staff should lift the one who is not wood!*

5 The peaceful kingdom   *Read Isaiah 11:1–9*

One of the features of the book of Isaiah that we may find confusing is the fact that very different themes and ideas follow one another in rapid succession. Thus, while earlier we were hearing about God's judgment on his people, now we hear about a very good and beneficial future for them. The present passage has a family likeness to the passage about the ideal king in 9:2–7. But we should also see it as coming after the harsh words about the king of Assyria in chapter 10. What we are being given in 11:1–9 is the confident and bold assurance that the days are surely coming when national life for the people of Judah and Jerusalem will be much better. But perhaps their country will not be as large as it was once: that would seem to be the meaning of the expression 'A shoot shall come out from the stump of Jesse'. But the talk seems to be of a new king of the line of David—for David was the son of Jesse of Bethlehem (1 Samuel 16).

Verse 2 speaks of a series of attributes that the king will have as a result of the gift of the spirit of the Lord. Without such a gift, no person would have such wisdom and understanding. And the whole of this person's life will be directed towards God. That is the meaning of the expression, 'His delight shall be in the fear of the Lord'. In the Old Testament, 'fear' is not the same as our 'being afraid', but it is a trembling awe before the mighty God, reverence before the majesty of the Lord. But the possession of these divine attributes will have a whole range of effects upon what he does in his life, and what he is able to do. These consequences are set out in verses 3–5. The final result of these good kingly and political actions and leadership for the people will be new realms of peace and harmony throughout the world. In fact it will be as it was intended to be at the very beginning. There will be a new Paradise (vv. 6–8).

The 'holy mountain' in verse 9 is presumably Zion and the city of Jerusalem. The expression, 'The earth will be full of the knowledge of the Lord as the waters cover the sea' is also found in Habakkuk 2:14 (perhaps quoting the Isaiah passage). This will be the work of God, and yet at the same time it will happen only when people turn to the Lord—when their 'delight shall be in the fear of the Lord'. Let that be our delight!

6   Thanksgiving and praise   *Read Isaiah 12:1–6*

This short chapter is in the style of the biblical psalms of thanksgiving. In fact, it is really two psalms of thanksgiving: the first, in verses 1–2, is from the lips of an individual person; the second, in verses 3–6, is an expression of thanks to God from a community of people. But it has surely been placed here at this point in the book as a way of rounding off a series of chapters that deal with a particular phase in the life of the people of Judah and Jerusalem. They have gone through many things, some of which we have been reading about in the passages we have studied. These people have sinned, and they have received the Lord's judgment at the hands of the king of Assyria. But all has not been gloom. There have been bold expressions of hope and confidence, and, in particular, wonderful pictures of those who one day will rule God's people with wisdom and understanding, in justice and righteousness. Now at the end of this series of passages about judgment and hope, there is this song of thanksgiving to God. Israel has been restored, and now the people give thanks.

Subsequent chapters of the book will take us into a wider world, in which the little nation of Judah is first caught up in a great ferment of nations, and is then portrayed as having her life assessed in a cosmic setting. But that lies, as it were, in the future. What is important in the present moment is to draw strength and hope from the experiences of the past, and, with the help of those experiences, to go in faith into the future. So the prophet calls his people to look back over the past years and all that they have brought, and to give thanks to God for his great mercies to them. And he gives to each member of the nation an expression of thanksgiving and commitment to utter:

> *Surely God is my salvation;*
> *I will trust and will not be afraid,*
> *For the Lord God is my strength and my might;*
> *He has become my salvation (v. 2).*

GUIDELINES

Before we move on into the wider world portrayed in the rest of Isaiah 1–39, we pause to look back on the passages we have read from chapters 1–12. After the opening chapter, which, as we saw, is perhaps intended as an introduction to the whole of the book, we have had a series of words mainly from the prophet Isaiah. These words came from the earlier periods of his ministry, in particular from the times before and during the so-called Syro-Ephraimite crisis when the little state of Judah was attacked by the coalition of the states of Israel and Syria. In these various passages we have been hearing a prophet speaking to his people about God.

The message has been above all about God. He is the great reality in the life of the world, and in the lives of its people. He is the Lord of all the earth, and in his great holiness he is separate from and different from all other beings. For Isaiah, this God is the 'Holy One', whose presence and hard reality should not be ignored by any.

But he is the God who is concerned about his people. He is the 'Holy One of Israel', and he calls for an answering response from his people, in terms of both worship and obedient living. As the Lord himself deals with his people in a context of justice and righteousness, so he calls for those things to be put into practice in the communal life of his people. When those people fail him, he must come in judgment. Yet he will also redeem, and he holds out for his people the promise of a good and hopeful future.

Then there is much about the prophet Isaiah in these chapters—one who was called by God to service, and sent to his people to speak the Lord's word to them. As we look back over the centuries, perhaps we may find ourselves wishing that the people had attended more wholeheartedly to God than they did. When God in his great goodness had sent a prophet to them to reveal God's will to them, why did they not listen, and act? But then, surely God continues to speak to *us* these days through his prophets, yet do we listen? Are we any better than those who went before us?

1–7 FEBRUARY   ISAIAH 13–27

1 God and Babylon *Read Isaiah 13:1–16*

Our readings today and for the three following days take us into the world of the nations. The Lord God may have been the 'Holy One of Israel', and we may rightly feel a sense that God is *our* God, and *my* God. Yet it is the wonder of the divine grace that the mighty Lord of all the nations cares for each one of us. Perhaps we can only appreciate the full wonder of that when we are confronted with the greatness of the Lord of the nations. Isaiah 13–27 is made up of a series of speeches about foreign nations, some coming from Isaiah, others from later times.

In Isaiah 13:2–3 the Babylonians are spoken of in favourable terms. God has a work for them to do: they have been chosen by God and are now consecrated to him. In verses 4 and 5 we have talk of war, and the meaning seems to be that these Babylonians are being summoned by the Lord. But this is something more than just a foreign army that is coming. This is nothing less than 'the Lord and the weapons of his indignation' (v. 5). That is, the Babylonian army is coming to fulfil God's will, to bring about a corrective to those affairs in the nation of Judah that are such an affront to the holiness and purity of God. This chapter may seem to us to be harsh and even heartless, but what it is doing is to take with the utmost seriousness the 'fierce anger' (v. 13) of God against human sin. In this advance of the Babylonian army there is portrayed the holy God confronting human wickedness.

It is tempting to see the New Testament as portraying a more loving God than the harsh one of the Old. Yet there is still in the New the Lord's judgment upon sin. What is new in the New Testament is that God himself provides the means whereby the world and its people may be redeemed from their sinful state. The Judge himself offers the means whereby his people may be set free from their sins. But perhaps we only come to appreciate the wonder of that message of the New Testament as we read and ponder the message of Isaiah and others in the Old.

2   Egypt converted!   *Read Isaiah 19:16–25*

This is a much more attractive passage for us than the one from Isaiah 13. How much more hopeful! In fact it is one of the most remarkable passages in the whole of the book of Isaiah—even in the whole of the Old Testament. It holds out for us the vision of God as the true Lord of all the nations. What is more, the nations acknowledge this. At least Egypt and Assyria do, and in the days of Isaiah those were by far the most significant and powerful nations. In comparison, Moab could do what it pleased!

The whole passage is made up of five small sections, each introduced by the expression 'on that day' (vv. 16, 18, 19, 23, 24), a phrase that indicates some indeterminate time—some stage in the future. And that is perhaps how we have to understand the passage: it is a vision of how things might be in the future, rather than the expectation of a series of events that will take place at particular historical moments. In all probability it comes from a time later than that of Isaiah, from the period after the Babylonian exile. But it makes a fitting conclusion to many of the things prophesied by Isaiah in his lifetime.

What a great change is envisaged as taking place in the national life of Egypt! First of all, the land that once had held the people of Israel captive (Exodus 1:8–14) will be made humble (vv. 16–17), and that clears the way for them to turn to worship the Lord—and to speak Hebrew (v. 18)! But more is to come: verses 19–22 speak of the conversion of the Egyptians to faith in Israel's God and of their acceptance of the rule of this God. It is further remarkable that Assyria is spoken about as turning to the Lord: as far as the Israelite people were concerned, Assyria was a most cruel and brutal nation (v. 23). Thus there will be a trio of nations—Egypt, Assyria and Israel—as good as equal (v. 24). Truly, nothing with God is impossible, and with prophets of old we must continue to dream dreams, and see visions, remembering that true word in Proverbs: 'Where there is no vision the people perish' (29:18, AV).

3 Jerusalem beware! *Read Isaiah 22:1–14*

Although the vision of Isaiah 19:16–25 encourages Jerusalem to look forward with confident hope to that day when the people and leaders of the great nations will regard her as an equal, still her people must recall that they themselves stand under the judgment of God. They are reminded (as we must be) that although they may be loved, protected and saved by the Lord God, they are still sinners. We must all never forget, 'For the time has come for judgment to begin with the household of God' (1 Peter 4:17).

The real sin of Jerusalem that has brought about these dire threats is various aspects of complacency. The emphasis in verses 1–4 is the cowardice and empty pride of the people; it seems that the city must have been under siege, but has not suffered defeat. It could be the event spoken of in 2 Kings 18:13ff, but the people are thinking that they themselves have done very well. In fact they surrendered to the enemy, but they fail to accept the reality of the situation. How we can all deceive ourselves! These people must take note of the great power, strength, and purpose of the Lord (vv. 5–7). More, they must in humility seek to gain something of that power and strength for themselves: as well as taking human action in the face of crisis, they must also 'have regard for him who planned it long ago' (vv. 8–11).

Verses 12–13 are about the people's complete mis-understanding of their real situation: instead of mourning, they are rejoicing. Instead of celebrating, they should be deeply concerned about all the suffering around them. The expression in verse 13, 'Let us eat and drink, for tomorrow we die' seems to have been a proverbial one, common at the time. The prophet sees his people's quoting it as symptomatic of their indifference to real life. But the prophet has heard a word from the Lord (as prophets do—Amos 3:7) and it is a very frightening word for these luxury-loving people (v. 14). The people may think that the attitudes they have adopted do not matter, and that the Lord will not act. But they do, and he will.

4 A corrupt official   *Read Isaiah 22:15–25*

Here we are introduced to two officials in Jerusalem, Shebna and Eliakim. First, there is Shebna, who is described both as steward and master of the household. That is, he holds high office in the royal palace, but clearly he has an over-exalted view of his own status, for he has prepared for himself a tomb in the special burial-place of Jerusalem kings. Such a person would expect to have a grave in the Kidron Valley, and in verse 16 he is warned that there will be an empty tomb amongst those of the kings (notice the emphasis in this verse on the 'here', three times!) that will be a lasting monument not to his own nobility and greatness, but to his overwhelming vanity. But his prepared tomb will be empty for another reason—that he will not die in Jerusalem, but far away in a foreign land (v. 18). This verse speaks about the man being rolled up as tight as a ball, and thrown away. We are intended to hear a play on words here: this action sounds rather like the binding up of a corpse in a long cloth wrapping. The message is that stewards of all people must remember their position, for stewards are not themselves owners, but rather are put in charge of other people's property.

Shebna's replacement is to be Eliakim, who will have all the trappings of office (v. 21), but, much more importantly, will be a 'father' to the people of Jerusalem. This is how a royal officer should behave. We may recall that Isaiah's ideal king was to be 'Everlasting Father' (Isaiah 9:6). Moreover (v. 22), he would have the key to the royal palace, a real symbol of his authority. This verse is quoted in Revelation 3:7, and we may recall the authority and the power of the keys that are given to the disciple Peter in Matthew 16:19.

The final verse is very different in tone, and was perhaps added at a later date, reflecting the time when the people of Judah and Jerusalem were in exile, again without king and royal officials. Still they waited for the true 'Everlasting Father' and those who would serve him, if not perfectly, at least in faithfulness and obedience.

5   The end of the world   *Read Isaiah 24:1–13*

The readings for today and tomorrow are from Isaiah 24–27, a series of chapters that deal with the theme of the end of the world. These chapters are different from other parts of the book both in the language they use, and also in their subject-matter. Both the language and the content are rather like those of the books of Daniel and Revelation, and Isaiah 24–27 is often called the 'Isaiah Apocalypse', rather in the same way that Mark 13 (a chapter of the Bible with the same sort of language and content) is sometimes called the 'Marcan Apocalypse'. One of the distinctive emphases of Apocalyptic is that things on earth are in a most desperate state, so serious that something much more is needed than the challenging words of a prophet. It needs nothing less than God to bring in a new order of things—and by direct action.

This explains why the present passage opens with such a seemingly harsh and violent sentence upon the whole of the earth (v. 1). The language of this verse may imply an earthquake, but equally it is clear that such an earthquake is portrayed not so much as a 'natural happening' but as the means that the Lord God employs in order to bring about the end of all things. The reason why things have gone so disastrously wrong is given in verse 5: it is because of the sinfulness of the people of earth. Those ways that God has given for people to follow have not been followed, and the 'covenant' relationship has been broken. In various places the Old Testament speaks of a covenant, that is, a relationship, between God and his people. Perhaps the thought in this passge is about the covenant that God made with all people after the time of the flood (Genesis 9:1–17).

Altogether it is a tragic and terrible scene that is portrayed here. The faithful city (Isaiah 1:21–26) will be devastated, or to use another image, it will be like an olive tree beaten in harvest time, like a vine being harvested. What we are being told is that very little will be left of the city.

6 Perfect peace *Read Isaiah 26:1–15*

The last passage from Isaiah that we read portrayed with devastating frankness the perilous situation of a world that does not look to God in obedience or turn to him for help and strength. Without God, his people are in a perilous situation. The present passage gives the other side of the matter, speaking about the strength and security that are to be found in God.

Verses 1–6 are in the form of a hymn of rejoicing. The singers marvel that they are part of a strong city; presumably the city is Jerusalem. Verse 2 pictures people who had in earlier times been scattered throughout the world, now coming in procession back to the chosen and holy city. We are reminded of the images of processions of people coming to Jerusalem in Psalms 15 and 24, and also in Isaiah 2:2–4.

In verse 3 comes a wonderful expression of the 'peace' that is to be found by those who put their trust in God. The original has '*shalom shalom*', and in the AV was translated memorably, 'Thou will keep him in perfect peace, whose mind is stayed on thee: because he trusteth in thee.' 'Peace' in the Old Testament is much more than the absence of warfare, strife and trouble, but indicates a setting of security, well-being, confidence, abundance, fulfilment. This blessed state is only attained by those who look wholeheartedly to God. The 'steadfast mind' refers to the whole direction and orientation of a person. The following verse, using a different image, makes clear the meaning of verse 3: those who put their trust in God will find in him the real 'rock' on which to build their lives (compare Matthew 7:24–25).

Verses 7–15 are not quite so straightforward, but they do seem to be speaking of two groups of people. There are those who look to God in trust and hope, relying upon him, even yearning for him, earnestly seeking him (v. 9). These are the ones who will know the true peace of God, and they will acknowledge that they owe this gift entirely to the Lord (v. 12). As far as the nation is concerned, it is God who has granted the success and the increase (v. 15). On the other hand are those who do not look to God, those who are proud of their own strength and achievements (vv. 10–11). For them, death will indeed be their end—the end not only of their physical presence on earth, but also of others' memory of them (v. 14).

GUIDELINES

Our readings this week have taken us into the setting of the world. Parts of the Isaiah book give us a very exalted picture of God as the Lord of all the world. His glory fills the earth (6:3), and in various ways he is involved in the lives of the nations. A later part of the book will tell how this same God called a great leader of another nation so that God's people could be rescued from their Babylonian captivity (45:1–7). This is the faith in which we live our Christian lives. We believe that God is the Lord of all creation, and that he sent his Son to save the world (John 3:16). Yet at the present time the world is turned away from God, and it is as if, to use the language of the apostle Paul, 'the whole creation has been groaning in labour pains until now' (Romans 8:22). But it will be the same for nations and individuals: their peace will be found only in God, the creator of all things and beings, the one true Lord of all. Evelyn Underhill (1875–1941), writing about the accounts of creation in the book of Genesis says this, and it is surely pertinent to what we have been reading:

So we dwell on this great picture of Creation, lying under the warm shadow of His wings: the quietness of the dark waters, those mysterious deeps with all their unrealized possibilities of life, beauty and power—and the patient, loving presence of God, the Perfect, Who, by His ceaseless action on the imperfect, alone gives form and brings forth life. We are not looking at something finished and done with; we look so far as we dare, at an Eternal process—the increasing actions of the Divine Love.

From Evelyn Underhill, Collected Papers of Meditations and Prayers, London, 1946.

8–14 FEBRUARY   ISAIAH 28–39

1   Woe to Jerusalem!   *Read Isaiah 29:1–8*

How do you explain a short passage in the Bible that begins with a prophecy of a devastating siege of Jerusalem but which quickly goes on to speak about the defeat of the besieging army and the deliverance of the besieged city? That is what we have to try to do with the present passage with its talk of siege in verses 1–4 and deliverance in verses 5–8. The first part is understandable, especially after what we have read so far in Isaiah: here is the prophet warning his people of an attack upon their city, no doubt because of the sin of its inhabitants. But here the city is known by a name that we do not otherwise encounter, 'Ariel'. This is a Hebrew word that seems to mean 'altar hearth', and is a reference to the altar of burnt offering that stood in the temple in Jerusalem. The threatening message in these verses is that the city itself is going to be like an altar hearth (v. 2)—the whole city will go up in smoke! Indeed, the Lord himself is pictured as being like the conqueror of Jerusalem, like young David of old (2 Samuel 5:6–10). The result of this will be that those who live in the city will die. They will go down into Sheol, the place where Hebrew people believed one went at death (v. 4).

Probably, the historical situation that lies behind this is the attack on Jerusalem by the Assyrian king Sennacherib in 701BC.

It is most likely that Isaiah 1:7–8 has the same background, and the reference there to 'daughter Zion' being 'left like a booth in a vineyard' is about Jerusalem alone being spared by the Assyrians while all the rest of the towns and cities of Judah fell to them. And indeed Jerusalem was spared (as we read in Isaiah 36–37), and to those who witnessed this remakable happening it did indeed seem 'miraculous'. That is perhaps how we are to take Isaiah 29:5–8, as a reflection on the remarkable—even 'miraculous'—fact that the city was spared. Surely, all of us feel that we have experienced mercies and deliverances that appear to us to have been 'miraculous'! Further, there is so much here of the message of the prophet Isaiah. God's own chosen city of Jerusalem (like his people) is not without sin, and yet he constantly delivers it, and has new purposes for it.

2 Doom… and glory! *Read Isaiah 29:9–24*

Once again we have a passage to read that threatens judgment upon God's people, but that also assures them of coming days of great glory. There is no denying the fact that verses 9–16 have a threatening aspect, and this is portrayed through three sayings (which perhaps came from three different occasions, and which have now been put together in the present passage). Each of these three sayings is about the folly of the leaders of the people. In verses 9–12 these leaders are condemned for their sleepiness: they are not awake to the realities of the situation around them. It has been suggested that the historical setting is that of the badly thought out policy of appealing to Egypt for help in the political crisis due to the threat from the Assyrians in 701BC.

The second word is also about blindness (vv. 13–14), but here the issue is about hypocrisy. These are people who are paying lip-service to God, but their hearts are far away from God. They are on their religious 'tramlines', just doing 'by rote' (v. 13) what should be a heartfelt and spiritually alive act of service. They are warned that God has some surprises in store for people who have got out of the habit of thinking imaginatively (v. 14)!

The third word is a condemnation of these who think that they can hide themselves and their decisions from God (vv. 15–16). But nothing can be hidden from God: he knows about everything that takes place. Indeed, for mere human beings to think that they can keep things secret from God is rather like suggesting that a clay pot can turn round to the potter who made it and tell him that he doesn't know what he is doing (v. 16)!

Surely such people must be beyond redemption! But no. There follow in verses 17–24 hopeful and confident words about a new future of blessedness and hope for these people. A day will come when human beings will act with new sense and openness, and there will also be a great renewal of nature. Further, all this will lead to a great renewal of worship—when people see what great things God has done, they will indeed 'stand in awe of the God of Israel' (v. 23). Even the grumblers will change their attitude (v. 24)!

3   Righteousness!   *Read Isaiah 32:1–8*

Here is a vision of an ideal future in which God is taken with the utmost seriousness, especially by national leaders. The Old Testament understands the importance of good political leadership. When this is lacking the people go astray. The Old Testament is neither afraid nor shy of criticizing the political leaders of the day. It is not in any way that religious people are dabbling in matters that are not their concern. These are God's people, and this is God's world, and how people live is very much God's concern. Thus, how people are led is also very much God's concern.

The wonderful promise here is that a day will dawn when the people will be led well, not only by the king, but also by those who rule with him (v. 1). The great benefit of such leadership is expressed in verse 2 in a series of pictures drawn from weather and the world of nature. Thus a good king and sound political leaders give shelter in the storms of life. The picture of the leaders of the people who are 'like the shade of a great rock in a weary land' is taken up in the hymn 'Beneath the cross of Jesus I fain would take my stand', as referring to the cross at Calvary. There indeed is the true place of help for God's people.

In this new era, people will pay proper attention to God's word, and to those who are wise (v. 3). Gone will be the days when people were unresponsive to God. People will be neither 'rash' (that is, hasty and unthinking in their speaking and decision-making), nor will they be 'stammerers' (that is, they will speak well—see Proverbs 18:21). Verse 5 speaks about the end of the era of fools—for the Old Testament, these are the people who are not fit to rule (see Proverbs again, 8:5; 9:4). The people of Israel had had their fair share of such rulers, and here they are promised a new and better day of leadership by those who are 'noble' and who plan and work 'noble' things (Isaiah 32:8).

And for that day we all long, not just that we alone may benefit, but that all may experience the protective presence of wise and caring leadership. Let the people of God pray and work for that in the world today!

4 Hezekiah's illness   *Read Isaiah 38:1–8*

Here we read about the sickness of an individual, in fact the king upon whom so much depended as regards the life and welfare of the whole nation. But we are not dealing with a 'bad' king here; far from it, for Hezekiah is portrayed as being pious. He appeals to his prophet Isaiah to help him, in particular to pray for him. Isaiah does this, with the result that the king recovers.

A number of aspects of this story should be noted. While it is surely right and reasonable that we should pray for people when they are ill, we should also remember that medical science has made enormous progress since the days of Hezekiah and Isaiah. There were very few 'doctors' in those days, and by our standards they knew very little. According to Ecclesiasticus 38:14 (found in the Apocrypha), physicians must rely on praying to God for their diagnosis of illness to be correct! So, while we pray about illness, let us also take what practical steps we can— and go to see the doctor. And thinking about that, we should note that this story of Hezekiah's illness is also told in 2 Kings 20:1–11, and that in that account some 'medical' details are included. In particular Isaiah tells the king's servants to apply a poultice of figs to the boil that was troubling the king (2 Kings 20:7). Thus, in that account, as well as prayer there is some action taken in the crisis.

Then this story tells us something about the reality of prayer. Here are people who have troubles and difficulties and they pray to God, who, although he may be the mighty Lord of heaven and earth, is also the God who invites his people to pray to him, and who also promises that he will hear them. Surely, Isaiah 38:5 (see also 2 Kings 20:5) is one of the most thrilling words of scripture with its assurance from God, 'I have heard your prayer'.

Finally, let us recall what a contrast there is between the attitude of this king Hezekiah in his time of crisis and that of his father Ahaz in his time of trouble. While Ahaz, lacking the spirit of faith and trust in God panicked (see Isaiah 7:2, 9), his son in quiet trust and confidence prayed to God (see Isaiah 30:15).

5   Hezekiah gives thanks   *Read Isaiah 38:9–20*

After the story of the illness and the promise of recovery of King Hezekiah (Isaiah 38:1–8), there now follows a psalm of thanksgiving. But the one feature conspicuous by its absence is any reference to Hezekiah and his illness! The psalm is a much more general expression of thanksgiving for deliverance, yet it is very appropriate in this place. It reminds us by its presence here that after prayer and deliverance there should come thanksgiving. Indeed, in our worship of God, prominence should be given to this note of thanksgiving. We acknowledge that we owe so much to God, and that without his constant help we would be in great difficulties. So we give thanks to God. And we have a psalm here to use in our thanksgiving to God. Further, in the Old Testament there are other psalms of thanksgiving, many of which are expressed in general terms. This is perhaps quite intentional: if they continued to have specific references to this situation or that, we would not be able to use them so readily. As it is, they seem to have been handed on to us in a form in which they can be used again and again by people in a whole range of different situations.

Verses 10–13 tell us of the king's desperate situation, and in graphic language express the thought that life could have come so easily and quickly to an end. Equally, these verses express the belief, common in much of the Old Testament, that there is no life after death, apart from the rather vague and shadowy life in the place of the dead, *Sheol*. The apostle Paul will come to see that in the new era of Christ we have great assurance (1 Corinthians 15:55).

But the king's trust is in God (v. 17), and when he experiences God's deliverance he turns to praise and thanksgiving (v. 19). Moreover, he now has a new confidence for the future, sure that in those crises yet to come to him he will again experience the delivering power of God—'The Lord will save me'. And he will be a singer of the praises of God for the rest of his life (v. 20)! What a fine example there is here for us all to follow!

6 What of the future? *Read Isaiah 39:1–8*

Isaiah 36–37 tells how the city and people of Jerusalem were delivered from the threat of the Assyrian army. The attacking army might have been very powerful, and the people of Jerusalem may have been very sinful, but God—the Holy One of Israel—had great plans and great works for his people to do. Thus the Lord delivered the city from its dangers.

But the fact is that eventually Jerusalem did fall to attackers. Although it was spared when the Assyrians attacked, at a later date the city fell to the Babylonians and many of the people were deported to Babylon. The passage that we read today was perhaps intended to go some way to make a 'bridge' from the time of deliverance from the Assyrians to that of captivity by the Babylonians. And the chapters in the book of Isaiah that follow will tell how God's people were rescued from their Babylonian captivity by God (chs. 40–55), and how their national life was re-established back in Israel (chs. 56–66). But here, in chapter 39, the issue is how God's people came to be carried away captive to Babylon, and why such a dreadful thing should happen when they were ruled by such a good king as Hezekiah.

The Babylonian king Merodach-baladan reigned from 721 to 710BC. The Assyrians were still the major power in Mesopotamia, but Merodach-baladan did his best to stir up revolts against Assyria. Presumably the reason for the visit of his envoys to Jerusalem was to enlist Hezekiah in his anti-Assyrian movement. And to Hezekiah these people do seem very friendly, but the prophet Isaiah is highly critical of his having given away the nation's secrets about its armoury and defences! So the prophet warns that, far from being an ally of Babylon, the day will come when the people of Jerusalem will be captives of the Babylonians (vv. 5–7). And that was a sad ending for the very fine and successful reign of Hezekiah, which had indeed brought great 'peace and security' to the nation through many days (v. 8). But we should bear in mind that, although this may be the final word in one part of the Isaiah book (chs. 1–39), it is by no means the final word of the whole book. There are whole new realms of 'peace and security' yet to come!

GUIDELINES

We have been reminded this week of a number of 'opposites' that the people of God experienced in times past—how their sinful city was judged, but how it was delivered; how they were 'ill' but how they were granted recovery. And we in our lives today experience such contrasts, and surely one of the reasons why the long and great book of Isaiah has been put together has been to help us deal with such seemingly contrasting, even conflicting, experiences of life. While we may not find it particularly difficult to see and to understand the presence of God with us in the good times, undoubtedly most of us find it much harder to know that God is with us in the bad times. These chapters of Isaiah have tried to show us, through the example of a series of historical events, that God is *always* with his people.

These chapters have also spoken to us of the reality of sin, yet at the same time giving us the assurance that, in spite of our sins, God still has purposes for us. He must judge us as sinners, and he must condemn the sin, but he still calls us to be his people and his servants. Jesus not only said, 'Your sins are forgiven' (Luke 7:48). He also said, 'Go your way, and from now on do not sin again' (John 8:11). And he also said, 'Follow me' (Mark 1:17).

A prayer of St Francis of Assisi (1182–1226):

Most high and glorious God, enlighten the darkness of our hearts and give us a true faith, a certain hope and a perfect love. Give us a sense of the divine and knowledge of yourself, so that we may do everything in fulfilment of your holy will; through Jesus Christ our Lord.

Further reading

R.E. Clements, *Isaiah 1–39*, New Century Bible Commentary, Eerdmans/Marshall, Morgan & Scott, Grand Rapids/London, 1980

J.F.A. Sawyer, *Isaiah*, Volumes I and II, The Daily Study Bible, Saint Andrew Press/Westminster, Edinburgh/Philadelphia, 1984, 1986

D. Stacey, *Isaiah 1–39*, Epworth Commentaries, Epworth Press, London, 1993

The Glory of the Lord

The readings for the next three weeks bring us into the beginning of Lent. They are about the glory of the Lord, made known to the people of God in three different contexts: (1) in the deliverance of the children of Israel from Egypt and their encounter with God at Mount Sinai; (2) in the experience of exile in Babylon, and the return to the promised land; (3) in the person of Jesus portrayed in the Gospel of Luke.

These notes are based on the Authorized Version of 1602: the beauty of that version is unchallenged, and for many of us it has been one of the main channels through which the glory of the Lord has been revealed to us.

15–21 FEBRUARY   THE GLORY IN THE EXODUS

The book of Exodus tells the story of the journeying of God's people from Egypt to the Promised Land. The story was at first handed down, no doubt, by word of mouth; but by the time the book reached its present form it had been reworked by several 'editors'. The latest of them represents what scholars call the Priestly Tradition—concerned above all with the *holiness* of God. This editor's hand is to be seen in most of this week's readings.

1   Vision and vocation   *Read Exodus 2:23—3:12*

Some of the older commentaries are very ingenious in trying to identify what kind of a bush this might be, and how it could burn without being consumed. If you're ever lucky enough to visit St Catharine's Monastery at the foot of Mount Sinai, you will be shown the site of this phenomenon, and a bush still growing on the spot. But you may feel that all this is beside the point. The significance of this event, surely, is that it marks the moment at which Moses, awestruck by a mysterious encounter, recognizes God's calling and responds to it.

Very often, in the Old Testament and the New, vocation is accompanied by vision. Isaiah in the temple, Paul on the

Damascus road—we know about their experiences because each told his own story. But the working of Moses' mind is almost entirely hidden from us. The scriptures portray him as a leader, a deliverer, whose authority even Pharaoh recognizes. But he doesn't go unchallenged among his own people. He has moments when he seems close to despair, when his anger breaks out against his followers and against God himself. Something about his origins made him almost an outsider in Israel: 'Who made *thee* a prince and a judge over us?' (Exodus 2:14). But of Moses it was said that God spoke to him 'as a man... unto his friend' (Exodus 33:11) and, rather surprisingly, that 'he was very meek, above all the men which were upon the face of the earth' (Numbers 12:3).

It's a complex picture. And the record suggests that it all springs from that moment at 'the backside of the desert' when God appeared to him, so mysteriously, in the bush that burned but was not consumed.

2   God's great work and our discomfort
Read Exodus 14:13—15:1

The deliverance of Israel, promised at the burning bush, is now realized at the Red Sea—deliverance for the children of Israel, death by drowning for Pharaoh and his army. Israel sees it as God's 'great work' (v. 31) and Moses sings his victory song to the Lord, the man of war, who has dealt gloriously.

You and I may not be very happy with this view of things. But we are struck with the fact that this triumph, this moment of deliverance, has always been celebrated by Jews and Christians as a key moment in the story of God's dealings with his people. These chapters are still read in many churches on and around Easter Day—hardly the moment (you'd think) to be gloating over the Egyptian dead. We're not so much inclined, as our forefathers sometimes were, to worship God as a man of war. But perhaps we shouldn't feel *too* smug about that. Our God is, after all, the God of Abraham, Isaac and Jacob, as Jesus reminds us (Matthew 22:32) and we can't distance ourselves completely from the triumphalism of the Old Testament. It's part of the rock from which we are hewn and the pit from which our faith has been dug (Isaiah 51:1). It comes into view again in the book of Revelation, and it is one way in which Israel saw the glory of the Lord. But I think we're right to feel uncomfortable about it in the face of Jesus Christ, the Prince of Peace.

3   Glory and terror   *Read Exodus 24*

The children of Israel were soon disheartened by their experience of the desert. And they were fed up with Moses, almost ready to stone him (Exodus 17:4). But on the third new moon after leaving Egypt they encamped at the foot of Mount Sinai. And there they received the commandments and the testimony. This was an encounter which, like the burning bush and the crossing of the Red Sea, was central to their understanding of God. It is part of our inheritance in faith, so that we can still sing,

> *O come, O come, Adonai,*
> *who in thy glorious majesty*
> *from that high mountain clothed with awe*
> *gave thy folk the elder law.*

Once again the context seems strange to us. Most of us haven't lived in the desert, other than the interior wilderness of our own hearts. And to all of us the idea of blood sacrifice is quite repugnant. But it was the natural response of an ancient people to the holiness and glory of the divine presence. We have to keep that in mind.

To the leaders of his people, and to seventy of the elders, there was more to come—something that breaks all the rules, so to speak, because it goes almost without saying, in the Old Testament and the New, that no one can see God and live. Yet here we read that 'upon the nobles of Israel he laid not his hand: also they saw God and did eat and drink' (v. 11).

In the closing verses of this chapter the glory of God is described in terms of pure terror. Moses alone goes into the cloud for six days of silence before the Lord speaks. Then comes the devouring fire, the purifying presence, and the long loneliness which (I suppose) comes to those very few to whom such a vision is granted. It may seem a different world from that other mountainside where Jesus preached, 'Blessed are the pure in heart: for they shall see God' (Matthew 5:8) but the vision is, in the end, the same. To be pure in heart is no easy matter.

4 'Shew me thy glory'   *Read Exodus 33:11–23*

Julian of Norwich was one of those of whom it could be said, as they said of Moses, that the Lord spoke to her 'as a man speaketh unto his friend'. She herself said, 'God willeth that we should be very homely with him, yet not so as to leave courtesy.'

Moses was courteous enough, up to a point. It was all very well, he suggested, for God to entrust him with the leadership of his people, and to assure him of his grace. But how was he to be sure of God's continuing presence? (Which of us hasn't at some time asked *that* question?) Then comes the outrageous demand: 'I beseech thee, shew me thy glory' (v. 18).

If the request was preposterous, the answer was breathtaking. The Lord would make his goodness to pass by, and would proclaim his name. He would not show his face, for that would be death to his friend; but he would hide Moses in a cleft of the rock and cover him with his hand as his glory passed by. Moses would see the back parts of God.

Amazing grace, indeed; and the echoes of God's friendship are heard now and again throughout the Bible. Think of Elijah cowering in his cave (1 Kings 19), of Jonah sulking in Nineveh (Jonah 4), of John in exile on Patmos (Revelation 1:9), and reflect on what it meant to them to be called the friends of God, to be covered with his hand, to espy his hinder parts.

5 Infectious glory   *Read Exodus 34:27–35*

There's no way we can get inside the mind of Moses. Our ways of thought and of speech are too different from those of the ancient Near East, and we remain strangers to the religious consciousness of those far-off times. We have to do our best with the wonderfully poetic accounts that they have left to us.

And so we read of Moses' great fast before God, a timeless encounter with the Most High, from which he comes back to earth (so to speak) bearing in his hands the very words that God has spoken to him. And he 'wist not that the skin of his face shone...' It's little wonder that Aaron and the rest of them were afraid to come near him. The Old Testament writers sometimes speak of holiness almost as if it were some kind of virus, something you could catch, which might destroy you if you came too close to it (see 2 Samuel 6:7). And here was Moses, their leader and colleague, a man who had been with them in all their wanderings, and now had been with God, and he was aglow with it. What was to be done about that shining face? Protection of some sort was called for, certainly: so let him veil his face when he spoke with the people, and uncover it when he went to speak with God.

Here, I think, is the first hint of a marvellous and alarming idea, that the glory of God was *communicable*; and even (later on) that a human life, your life or mine, could glorify God. This is what lies behind Paul's startling words about the unveiled presence of God before which 'we all, *with open face* beholding as in a glass the glory of God, are changed unto the same image from glory to glory, even as by the Spirit of the Lord' (2 Corinthians 3:18).

6 Glory in concealment *Read Exodus 40:34–38*

'So Moses finished the work' (v. 33). The compilers of the book of the Exodus have just devoted six long chapters to telling us what that work was; how the tabernacle was made, which was to be the model for the temple itself. We can read of those craftsmen with the wonderful names, Bezaleel and Aholiab, who made the sumptuous things for the place of meeting—the holy garments in purple and scarlet, with onyx stones set upon them, 'the pots, the shovels, the basins' in bronze, which the people offered for the service of the sanctuary—all the opulence which seemed proper for the worship of God.

But alongside all of that, there is the stark grandeur of the very last verses of Exodus. The glory of God, glimpsed at the burning bush, experienced on the holy mountain and from the cleft in the rock, manifested to the people by the shining of Moses' face, is now to be known not by revelation but in *concealment*. 'A cloud covered the tent of the congregation… and the glory of the Lord filled the tabernacle' (v. 36). Moses couldn't go in until the cloud lifted. Only when it did lift could the children of Israel resume their journeying.

God's people have to learn that the presence of God, the *glory* of God, is to be found not only in the brightness of vision but in the cloud which obscures it. The learning comes perhaps in the desert, certainly in journeying, as we follow the Way.

John Newton's 'Glorious things of thee are spoken' seems to be a hymn about the city of God. It is also about the exodus— the rock of ages, the streams of living water, the pillar of fire and the manna—and it has these fine words:

Round each habitation hovering,
see the cloud and fire appear
for a glory and a covering,
showing that the Lord is near.

A glory and a covering. A contradiction? A paradox? It could be simply true that the glory of God, 'his presence and his very self', is most surely to be known when it is most obscured, veiled, hidden from sight, only the back parts visible.

GUIDELINES

Franz Josef Haydn often wrote at the top of his compositions the letters A.M.D.G.—*Ad Majorem Dei Gloriam*, 'To the Greater Glory of God'. It's hard to think of a better dedication for our daily work, our daily reading, our fumbling attempts to live more closely with our Lord; or of a better 'arrow prayer' for Lent than this:

Glory be to the Father, and to the Son, and to the Holy Ghost:
as it was in the beginning, is now, and ever shall be, world
without end, Amen.

Perhaps in your own experience there is something to set beside what you've been reading this week:

- *an unexplained mystery, like the burning bush*
- *a moment of deliverance, as at the Red Sea*
- *a time in the wilderness*
- *God's friendship, veiled or revealed*

All of these may be (or should be) to the greater glory of God.

22–28 FEBRUARY · THE GLORY IN EXILE AND RETURN

The readings this week dodge about through various books of the Old Testament. This may irritate some of you, but there's a good reason for it.

In ancient times there were two key moments in Jewish history. First, the exodus: this has a book to itself, which we considered last week, and the account in it is fairly easy to follow. Second, the exile and return: it's much more difficult to trace this story, because the records are to be found in many different parts of the Old Testament and are quite hard to disentangle. Here's an over-simplified version.

In 722BC Assyrians conquer the Northern Kingdom of Israel, destroy its capital at Samaria, and carry its people into captivity (see the books of Kings and Chronicles). About 120 years later, Babylonians conquer the Southern Kingdom of Judah, take some of its inhabitants captive to Babylon and set up a puppet king in Jerusalem. Ten years after this, Judah rebels, Jerusalem is destroyed and an even larger part of its population deported (see Kings, Chronicles and Jeremiah). After seventy years of Jewish exile (see Ezekiel) the king of Persia, having conquered Babylon, allows some of the Jews to return to Jerusalem (Isaiah 40—55, Ezra, and Nehemiah). Several leaders emerge. The 'returners' are generally at odds with 'the people of the land' who hadn't been in exile. Jewish/Samaritan hostility is attributable partly to this. The walls and the temple are rebuilt (Haggai and Zechariah). The religion and the politics of the Jews become increasingly exclusive.

Many of the Psalms come from this period of exile and return. So does the 'editing' of earlier historical accounts such as Exodus.

1 Glory in a strange land   *Read Ezekiel 1:1–3 and 1:22—2:3*

This prophet was also a priest, and it shows. His upbringing, his service of the temple and its ceremonies, the mercy-seat and its attendant seraphim, the fires of its altars and the smoke of its incense—all this is clearly reflected in the imagery through which the vision of God's glory comes to him.

Ezekiel is very long-winded and repetitive. His imagination is feverish to the point of hysteria. It's often hard to discover when his mind is engaged with the realities of his exile (he was probably one of those taken in the first Babylonian captivity) and when he is transported in spirit to the temple that he knew, now in ruins, or to the restored temple which he longed to see. Many of the later chapters of his book are taken up with God's requirement of a new spirit among the shepherds of his people (chapters 34–36) and his promise of restoration (the valley of the dry bones in chapter 37).

In some famous words of Psalm 137, a poet of the exile asks, 'How shall we sing the Lord's song in a strange land?' It was an impossibility. Ezekiel, prophet and priest, would have felt the same. But the word comes to him in Babylon and a vision to go with it. What is that vision? It is a manifestation of the glory of the Lord. In that filthy, heathen place of idolatry and punishment the glory is revealed, unthinkably, unmistakably, hovering over the people of God.

The prophet falls on his face in wonder. He is told to stand upon his feet, to fulfil his mission to a degraded, disobedient, hard-hearted people. As far as we know, he ended his days in Babylon. But he had seen the glory.

2 Hope and glory   *Read Psalm 102*

There are some psalms which quite obviously date from the years of the exile: 'By the rivers of Babylon' (Psalm 137); 'Jerusalem a heap of stones' (Psalm 79). These are outpourings of grief for the destruction of the holy places.

Psalm 102 probably comes from those years, though scholars aren't unanimous about that. It is certainly a poem of lamentation, but in a Hebrew poem you can't always tell whether the grief is that of an individual, or whether the poet has become the representative voice of some national catastrophe.

What is special in this psalm is the middle part, verses 12–22. The groaning and misery suddenly give way to a hymn of hope and praise. Indeed, some commentators think that these verses belong to a different poem altogether; but that needn't be the case. If there's one thing that emerges from the bitterness of Jewish experience, it is that the people of God are those who 'going through the vale of misery, use it for a well: and the pools are filled with water' (Psalm 84:6 in Coverdale's translation).

Ezekiel was amazed to find the glory of the Lord revealed in the strange land. The psalmist, whatever form his afflictions may have taken, declares, 'When the Lord shall build up Zion, he shall appear in his glory' (v. 16). He is determined that 'this shall be written for the generation to come'. His vocation is 'to declare the name of the Lord in Zion, and his praise in Jerusalem'.

The AV and the RSV both translate this in terms of a *future* hope. Other versions use the past tense to describe the glory *as having already appeared*. It's sometimes quite difficult to tell the time in Hebrew! Perhaps T.S. Eliot's famous lines are appropriate to all expectation of the glory of the Lord:

Time present and time past
Are both perhaps present in time future,
And time future contained in time past.

From Burnt Norton, 1935

3   Glory, triumph and tenderness   *Read Isaiah 40:1–11*

When the Jews were in exile they could hardly avoid becoming familiar with the 'highways' of the Babylonian gods. A part of one of them is still preserved in a museum in Berlin: a processional entrance-way lined with glazed tiles in a stunning shade of blue, with heraldic beasts on guard. Along this triumphal route Marduk, or some such god, made his progress through the city with the acclamation of the multitudes.

What made the exile especially horrible to the Jews was the dreadful thought that here, outside the boundaries of the Promised Land, the children of Israel might conceivably be beyond the reach of their God. Could it be possible that by the waters of Babylon his authority no longer held good?

Today's reading is thoroughly familiar to us as the opening of Handel's *Messiah*. It incorporates a text quoted by John (John 1:23) and applied to the coming of the Baptist. It comes from Second Isaiah, as the scholars call him; and it begins with a word of 'comfort', a strengthening word to reassure the exiles that their God had by no means deserted them. They were to lift up their voices in welcome as the Lord made *his* triumphal progress—not through the streets of the abominable city but (as had been the case in that earlier exodus long before) straight across the desert.

It's easy to miss this point because the Greek version of the Old Testament, from which John quotes, is followed in most English versions of Isaiah 40. 'A voice crying in the wilderness' has become an English cliché. But the original Hebrew prophecy should properly be interpreted like this:

> *A voice cries: 'In the wilderness prepare a way for the Lord; make straight in the desert a highway for our God.'*

Ezekiel saw the glory of the Lord in his captivity. The psalmist saw past and future glory fulfilled in the restoration of Zion. Isaiah here proclaims a triumphal journey through the desert. 'The glory of the Lord shall be revealed', not only through the vision of his greatness, but by the showing forth of his tenderness, as the Shepherd of Israel once again gathers his flock into his arms.

4 Glory, praise and grief *Read Ezra 3:10–13*

Ezra the scribe came back from exile in the company of that shadowy figure Sheshbazzar, Prince of Judah, and was evidently a man of great influence among the returning Jews. He was certainly also a holy terror to the 'people of the land' who had not been taken away to Babylon. The books of Ezra and

Nehemiah show him to have been quite ruthless in prescribing how the law was to be kept and how the purity of the holy people was to be maintained. There was to be a purge of priests and other officials. Strict laws were enforced against mixed marriages and sabbath-breaking. All foreign influences were to be rooted out. At times it makes the blood run cold.

But here in these verses is a moment of extraordinary insight. The foundation stone is laid and the restoration of the temple begun. Soon they will be able to worship once again in the house of the Lord, a place fit for the celebration of his glory. However, there are mixed emotions, as always when religious feelings run high. There is a lot of noise. And in the din you couldn't tell who was cheering and who was weeping—weeping because the new brought back such distressing memories of the old.

Wherever there's progress, you get a sense of loss. It can be very painful when old traditions are replaced by new building, fresh insights. Listen to people talking of the 16th-century Reformation, of the Second Vatican Council, of any change in religious practice, and you'll find yourself wondering who's cheering and who's crying—and you have to hope that neither the oldies nor the youngsters, as emotions are aroused and parties formed, lose sight of the glory of the Lord who is God of the highway in the desert, and of the gathered flock, as well as Lord of the glorious temple.

5 Glory at the end   *Read Haggai 2:1–9*

Now that you've taken the trouble to find Haggai, among the farther reaches of your Old Testament, you could do worse than read it through. It's a fiery little book and it puts flesh, so to speak, on the dry bones of the return from exile.

Ezra was a scribe of the law. Haggai was a prophet and a poet and a visionary. The contrast between the old temple and the new, which caused such a commotion at the laying of the foundation stone, is now considered against a wider background.

Haggai looks *back* to the deliverance from Egypt (v. 5) and he sees in that experience what the Jews have always seen in it: the continuing, covenanted presence of the Lord through his spirit abiding with them. He also looks *forward*, as the prophets had done since the days of Amos 200 years earlier, to the Day of the Lord, to the 'end time' which paradoxically is also seen to be close at hand. This 'eschatological dimension' (from the Greek *eschaton*, 'end'), as it's called, becomes strong in the closing pages of the Old Testament (in Daniel, for instance) and it runs like a thread throughout the New.

The message, crudely speaking, is that the end is always near. The Day of the Lord, the kingdom of heaven, the parousia of Jesus (sometimes misleadingly called the second coming), are all ways of proclaiming faith in the God who is Alpha and Omega, the beginning and the end. And here Haggai places his perception of the glory of the Lord in the framework of a revelatory or *apocalyptic* vision (from the Greek *apokalypsis*, 'revelation'). 'It is a little while, and I will shake the heavens, and the earth…'.

It's almost as though a bridge is being built by which we can cross over from the religion of old Israel into the more familiar world-view of Jesus and the gospels. I say it is familiar. It ought to be. It remains none the less strange. Even now, when people talk glibly of Apocalypse and thrill themselves with sci-fi fantasies, it doesn't come naturally to expect a calamitous end of time which is also a manifestation of God's glory and a promise of peace. That's how this prophet saw it; and in his vision it is a promise not only to the Jews, but to the world.

The glory of the Lord is the desire of all nations.

6   **Radiant glory**   *Read Isaiah 60*

From the closing chapters of Isaiah (scholars refer to Isaiah 56—66 as 'Third Isaiah') come some more words familiar to lovers of oratorio. It is, by the way, an intriguing fact that in Handel's *Messiah* the story of the birth, death and resurrection of the Saviour is nowhere directly told. Indeed, the name of Jesus occurs only once, in the formal phrase 'through Jesus Christ our Lord'. It's amazing how much can be told, obliquely, in the words of those who went before and those who came after—

guided by the Spirit 'who spake by the prophets' and still does.

Isaiah 60 is a further enlargement of the vision of the glory of the Lord. It encompasses those who sit in darkness—Gentiles who come from afar on their dromedaries, with their gifts and their flocks. They come 'with acceptance' and God is glorified by their coming. Is this, I wonder, the beginning of a new understanding by which it dawns upon us not only that God is glorious, but that *we can glorify God*? It sounds like a great impertinence, but the New Testament is full of it.

Isaiah's teaching in these chapters isn't quite as rosy as it seems. Certainly the Gentiles have their part in the new dispensation; but they come into it rather low down the pecking order. They are to bring tribute, to serve the people of the covenant. 'The sons of strangers shall build up thy walls … the sons also of them that afflicted thee shall come bending…' (vv. 10, 14). The boot is on the other foot, and about time too.

It is a radiant picture, all the same: an apocalypse of hope and glory to set beside so much in scripture that foretells woe, and so much in human history that chronicles suffering.

GUIDELINES

What can I learn from the Jewish experience of exile and return? Here are some hints on self-examination for those of us who hope to keep Lent as a time for growth and renewal.

- *Can I find evidence of God's glory in unexpected places (the Ezekiel question)?*

- *What rebuilding needs to be done in my life and in my relationships (the Haggai question)?*

- *Can I be more aware—with help from my friends—of when I am too strict with myself and other people, and when I am not strict enough (the Ezra question)?*

- *Anxiety can be a crippling distraction—dwelling too much on time past, too much concern about time future. How open am I to God's grace in time present (the psalmist's question)?*

If you want a fully developed account of the glory of God as it is shown forth in the life of Jesus, and more particularly in his death, you need to study John's Gospel. There you will find, as a recurrent theme, the Lord's insistence that it is by the cross that the Son of Man is glorified.

That theme will be fully explored in the readings for Holy Week and Easter. So for this coming week we turn our attention not to John but to Luke. The readings will be taken from different moments in the third Gospel's account of the life of Jesus and will finally consider a text from Luke's second volume, the Acts of the Apostles.

1   Embodied glory   *Read Luke 2:8–20*

There can't be much in these wonderful verses that you haven't thought about and read about before. Christmas cards and carols and sermons all love to dwell on the shepherds in the fields and the message of the angels. How familiar it all is—and yet how strange!

In his commentary, C.F. Evans says that up to this point the birth narrative has been simply factual; now it becomes a matter of revelation. The glory of Christ's birth is, I suppose, not visible to the naked eye. It needs the message of the angels before the shepherds, or any of us, can recognize what is being done. It is something so blazing with light that they were, of course, sore afraid as the glory shone round them.

It is, first, a revelation *to all people*, good news that is universal, yet localized in this place, by the birth of this child. 'Let us now go… and see this thing which is come to pass, which the Lord hath made known unto us' (v. 15).

It is a revelation of *peace on earth*. That means, says John Tinsley, more than the absence of strife: it is 'entire harmony of life which, in its perfection, only God has … God's peace is God's alone, and it is his *favour* to men to bring about in them a peace which has some resemblance to his own.'

'Glory to God *in the highest*.' The glory of the Lord is celestial. It belongs to the eternal, uncreated being of the Most High. That can be dimly understood by anyone who cares to enquire into such matters. But what astonishes us about the gospel is here set before us at the start, in the message of the angels: that the glory is to be incarnate, *embodied* in the person of that child, born today. Those are the good tidings of great joy, which the shepherds were to 'make known abroad'.

'But Mary kept all these things, and pondered them in her heart' (v. 19). Hers, surely, were the sharpest ears and the clearest eyes, that night. The message can only, in the end, lodge in the hearts and minds of the humble and the obedient. 'Blessed are the pure in heart: for they shall see God' (Matthew 5:8).

2 Trinitarian glory   *Read Luke 4:1–15*

In writing his gospel, Luke apparently had access to material which the other evangelists either didn't know about, or didn't choose to include in their accounts. Some of this material is of outstanding value: the good Samaritan, the prodigal son, Dives and Lazarus—these we owe entirely to Luke. And there are less obvious ways in which he enriches our understanding of the life of our Lord.

In his account of the temptation he alone makes the point (v. 6) that the tempter presumes to offer Jesus *power and glory*. The word for 'power' implies 'authority'; and in human terms this in turn implies the ability to rule, to dominate in the affairs of men and nations. The devil supposes himself able to offer Jesus a share in this power, if he will worship him. This glory is for sale.

If you look forward from this moment of testing in the wilderness, it's not long before you realize how very different is the true glory of the Son of Man. Having resisted the temptations of the devil, he returns in the power of the Spirit into Galilee, where he preaches and teaches, 'being glorified of all' (v. 15). His authority is at once recognizable, before any signs and wonders have been recorded, because of 'the gracious words which proceeded out of his mouth' (4:22). As his work of healing began, the devils and the unclean spirits, too, recognized his authority, the true power and glory that comes only through the operation of the Holy Spirit of God.

The glory of God, shown by the power of the Spirit in the person of Jesus—it would be many years before the doctrine of the Holy Trinity found its place in the understanding of Christian people, but here it is already, in essence, at the very start of the gospel. Luke's great design, carried through in Acts to encompass the experiences of the apostles and the early church, was above all to show the power of the Spirit at work in the Saviour and in all who were to call upon his name.

3 Transfigured glory   *Read Luke 9:28–36*

We saw yesterday how Luke, in his account of the temptation, brings his own special insights to bear on the concepts of power, authority and glory. He tells of the transfiguration in much the same way, using the same tradition as Mark and Matthew, but treating it with some small but significant differences.

For instance, the first three evangelists (John doesn't tell of the transfiguration) all say that the disciples were *afraid*. Mark doesn't specify exactly what frightened them; presumably it was the whole experience of that mountain-top. Matthew says it was the voice from heaven that made them afraid. Luke says it was the cloud that overshadowed them: 'and they feared as they entered into the cloud' (v. 34). This, surely, is an echo of what we read in Exodus about the glory and the covering, the revelation of God that comes about in darkness and obscurity. Of course they were afraid!

Another instance: verses 31 and 32 have no parallel in the other Gospels. Only Luke says that Moses and Elijah 'appeared in glory'. Only Luke suggests what it was that Jesus had to say to them, that he 'spake of his decease which he should accomplish at Jerusalem'. And the word translated here as 'decease' is the Greek word *exodos*. There can be little doubt that Luke is pointing both *back* to the deliverance brought about by the exodus, and *forward* to the greater deliverance to be achieved on the cross. Both are revelations of the glory of the Lord.

'Peter and they that were with him were heavy with sleep: and when they were awake, they saw his glory, and the two men that

85

stood with him' (v. 32). There's reassurance for all of us in the weakness and vulnerability of Jesus' disciples, so often underlined in the gospels. They tend to drop off. But when they come to, they see his glory. Not only that: they see that when he emerges from the fearful cloud there are men standing with him in glory. And so it will always be, because of the exodus that he accomplished at Jerusalem.

4   Gratitude and glory   *Read Luke 17:7–21*

As you read the New Testament, and the commentaries and sermons that expound it, you get the idea that leprosy was a common condition in Palestine during Jesus' ministry. No doubt it was, but it's strange that John makes no mention of it. The other evangelists do, and Luke (the beloved physician?) has this additional incident which the others do not have.

The story is most beautifully told. It should, of course, be read in context. Jesus has been talking about faith and repentance and gratitude, and goes on to talk about the kingdom; and this healing of the ten lepers is set into that discourse like a small jewel of humanity in the great golden chain of the divine plan.

The healing, of course, is an act of compassion and a sign of the Lord's healing power. In an earlier miracle (Luke 5:13 and parallels) Jesus lays his hand upon the leper and heals him. In this incident much can be made of the fact that there is no physical contact—were they *all* Samaritans?—but that they were told to go to the priest, leprous as they were; and 'as they went, they were cleansed'. Their obedience was, to say the least, contributory to their cure.

One of the ten came back to give thanks. Not only that: *he gave glory to God*. And in so doing (if we take this point) he was not only cleansed but 'made whole'.

Preachers have a habit of taking small details of the gospel and blowing them up until they become grotesque. Perhaps one can make too much of these verses. But it can be said that Luke is the most moralistic of the gospel writers; and it would be in character for him to suggest that the simple ethical requirement of gratitude is one step towards an awareness of the glory of the Lord. Not only that: it enables you to 'give glory to God', which is an astonishing thing to be able to do. For this Samaritan leper, it seems to have been just so.

5 A procession into glory *Read Luke 19:29–40*

If the Samaritan leper got it right, are we to say that the crowd of Jews at the Passover got it wrong?

There is a great deal of discussion among scholars about the triumphal entry into Jerusalem. It revolves around what is called the 'messianic expectation'. We all know that the life of Jesus was lived among men and women who looked forward with passionate eagerness to 'the consolation of Israel' (Luke 2:25). Messiah would come and all would be well. But what form, exactly, did this expectation take? I think it must be said that different people had wildly differing hopes and aspirations which we can only partly understand. And therefore it is difficult for us now, and was probably difficult for them then, to decipher the signals which, according to the Gospels, Jesus was giving during these last days to his disciples, to the Jewish leadership, to the Romans, to the crowds.

For the moment, at any rate, the crowd was giving glory to God. According to Matthew (21:4) they interpret his arrival as the fulfilment of prophecy (Zechariah 9:9). Whether for religious or for political reasons, they believe the hour of deliverance may have come at last, and they give him a royal welcome: 'Blessed be the King that cometh in the name of the Lord: peace in heaven, and glory in the highest' (v. 38). This is different from the cry of 'Hosanna' that you find in Mark and Matthew. It's the message of the angels to the shepherds, gone wonky.

The Pharisees are horrified. Only Luke records this and Jesus' reply to them. Matthew tells of a rather different incident in the temple itself. The signals are indeed ambiguous. Not until John came to write the fourth gospel was it clear that the road to Calvary was the path of glory. But already in Luke (24:26), as the risen Christ walks with his friends to Emmaus, it is evident that the triumphal entry into Jerusalem had indeed been Messiah's procession into glory in a way that the crowds could not begin to imagine.

6 A witness to glory *Read Acts 6:8–15 and 7:54–60*

For our last reading we move into the second volume of Luke. The pivot between the two parts of his work is, of course, the coming of the Holy Spirit upon the assembly of the faithful at Pentecost. That is the fulfilment of the Good News, and the seal set on the community of the new Israel.

Stephen is the first member of that community to bear witness by his death. He is 'full of faith and power' (6:8). His wisdom and his spirit are irresistible (6:10). His opponents, 'looking steadfastly on him, saw his face as it had been the face of an angel' (6:15). We are reminded inescapably of Moses and his shining countenance.

The bulk of chapter 7 is given to Stephen's interpretation of the Old Testament as a record of Jewish disobedience. 'Ye do always resist the Holy Ghost: as your fathers did, so do ye' (7:51). This is too much. The Jews gnashed their teeth. Stephen, 'full of the Holy Ghost, looked up steadfastly into heaven, and saw the glory of God, and Jesus standing on the right hand of God' (v. 55). What he saw he told, and this to Jewish ears was blasphemy. There was no need for a formal sentence of death. The first Christian martyr is lynched by a devout mob.

As he dies, Stephen, like his Lord, yields up his spirit and forgives his killers. So we end this series of readings about the glory of the Lord. We see that glory communicated (if that's the right word) to the disciple by the grace of God and by the example and efficacy of Jesus' saving death and resurrection, and by the coming of the Spirit. The testimony which begins with a burning bush ends with a mangled corpse and a liberated spirit. To read this testimony, to reflect on it and pray about it, is to discover not only how glorious our God is, but how much of his glory he shares with his creatures through the outpouring of his Spirit, and how graciously he allows us in our small measure to glorify him.

The Spirit of God which brooded over the waters of creation breathes throughout the pages of Luke's two volumes as he traces the life of Christ and his legacy to his followers.

I think we greatly impoverish our prayers and our whole discipleship if we lose sight of this trinitarian dimension. It's no mere pedantry to say that all prayer is rightly offered to the Father through the Son in the fellowship of the Holy Spirit. It grates on the ear when public prayer is offered indiscriminately to somebody called 'Lord'. Private prayer, too, ought to be scrupulous in its address.

How pompous that sounds! However, here are some points for scrutiny:

- *I might consider my baptism as admission into those who hear the message of the angels.*

- *What power I have—and it may be considerable in the family, at the workplace, in the church—must be directed always to the glory of the Lord.*

- *The apostles were fearful in the presence of the transfigured Lord. Quite right, too.*

- *Why doesn't my face shine?*

Further reading

Two great books on the subject are out of print, but enthusiasts will find them in libraries. They are Arthur Michael Ramsey, *The Glory of God and the Transfiguration of Christ*, and David Jenkins, *The Glory of Man*.

Two excellent books, more easily accessible, are W. David Stacey, *Groundwork of Biblical Studies*, and John Tinsley, *Luke* (Cambridge Bible Commentary).

A larger and very splendid commentary on Luke is C.F. Evans, *Saint Luke* (TPI New Testament Commentaries).

*If you enjoy your Guidelines
Bible reading notes, why not consider
giving a gift subscription to a friend
or member of your family?*

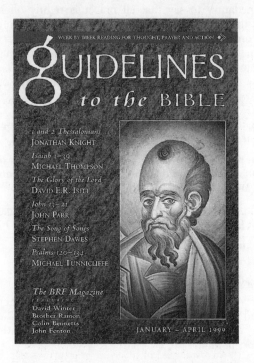

*You will find a gift subscription order form
on page 156.*

*You will find a gift subscription order form
on page 156.*

The Gospel of John
Chapters 13–21

The first half of John's Gospel covers a period of at least two years (three Passovers), but chapters 13—21 are devoted to a matter of weeks (13—20 to a single week). Time slows right down for the hour of Jesus' lifting up.

At the heart of these chapters lies Jesus' so-called Farewell Discourse, comparable to Jacob's farewell to his twelve sons in Genesis 49 and Moses' final words to Israel in Deuteronomy 31—34. Jesus prepares the disciples for a future in which 'you will not see me'. The discourse is framed by two actions. First there is Jesus' washing of the disciples' feet, which sets the tone for the teaching that follows. And then there is Jesus' crucifixion, in which he is not merely a passive victim but plays an active part. The first symbolizes the second: together they constitute Jesus' 'hour', to which the gospel has been pointing since the wedding at Cana.

The notes are based on the Revised Standard Version.

8–14 MARCH   **JOHN 13:1—14:31**

1   **To the feet of the disciples**   *Read John 13:1–11*

Mention of the Passover recalls the earlier Passovers when Jesus spoke of the temple of his body (2:21), and promised to give his flesh for the life of the world (6:51). Jesus is about to build a new holy place, in which sanctity is redefined as the self-giving love that takes him to his crucifixion. From here on the narrative is heavy with the anticipation of Jesus' death. It is the 'hour' that was first signalled in his words to his mother at the wedding in Cana (2:4); the hour 'when I am lifted up from the earth, (to) draw all men to myself' (12:32); the hour of his departure 'out of this world to the Father'.

This hour is characterized by 'love… to the end' (v. 1), and its movement 'from God … to God' is symbolized by the incident found only in this gospel, the foot-washing. Jesus 'laid aside his (outer) garments' in order to wash his disciples' feet, only to 'take' them again (vv. 4, 12). The language recalls the good shepherd's laying down his life and taking it again (see 10:11ff). We can picture Jesus descending to the disciples' feet before ascending to his place at table once more.

The image of Jesus acting out the role of the servant contrasts sharply with Judas: the icon of holiness alongside the instrument of the evil one. Judas is always associated in this gospel with betrayal (6:71; 12:4), but only now does the devil enter the picture. The actions of Judas and Jesus are intimately linked: one man's evil deed serves another's act of love. We are on the threshold of mystery, as God draws the darkness of evil into his redeeming work.

Presumably the disciples are surprised, and even embarrassed, by Jesus' servility. Only Peter objects, but his opposition evaporates at the thought of having 'no part in me'. The prospect of being excluded from Jesus' fellowship provokes the opposite reaction: 'not my feet only, but (wash) my hands and my head' (v. 9). Later, Peter and the others will understand the real significance of the foot-washing. Only by letting themselves be drawn into the humility of Jesus will they be able to share in the benefits of his passion.

The foot-washing replaces the institution of the Lord's supper in this gospel (the eucharistic words are brought forward to chapter 6, the discourse that follows the feeding of the five thousand). Water and cleansing are a reminder of baptism. Jesus' symbolic gesture reveals the true sense of the church's sacraments. More than empty religious rites, they dramatize the essence of Christian living: belief in Jesus as the one sent by God (see chapter 3), life nourished by his costly sacrifice. 'Clean' feet stand on holy ground.

2 At table once more *Read John 13:12–20*

The act which symbolizes Jesus' own humility is also a call to live by his generous love. Notice how Jesus draws on the hierarchical images of his world—teacher–disciple, master–servant, ruler–

emissary—to impress the pattern of his life on to that of his followers. But we should not lose sight of the way Jesus subverts traditional hierarchy. He is teacher, Lord and master *as servant*. This is how he represents the one who has sent him. And this is also how his followers represent him. The servant washing his disciples' feet, the man stripped of his clothes on the cross: these are icons of divinity and holiness, staking out holy ground and extending sanctity into the world through those who are 'chosen' and 'sent'.

Not all who are 'chosen' are 'sent'. 'You are clean, but not every one of you (v. 10) ... I know whom I have chosen' (v. 18). Judas is a counter-example of sanctity understood as self-giving service, the antitype of discipleship. His impending act of treachery fulfils the scripture—the whole of Psalm 41:9 is worth recalling: 'Even my bosom friend in whom I trusted, who ate of my bread, has lifted his heel against me'—but we should not imagine that Judas merely acts out a script written for him in advance. The evangelists are not interested in the reasons for Judas' betrayal, and leave only a few tantalizing clues. The note of fulfilment here underlines the authority of Jesus who 'knows', something the disciples will recognize later, 'when it does take place' (with the promise of later understanding in verse 19, cf. v. 7).

'One *of you* will betray me' (v. 21). Sharing a meal meant more than refreshing the body, or even enjoying the company of others. The meal table symbolized the sacred bonds joining one to another. To share table fellowship was to offer life to others. Breaking it meant withdrawing life—here to the extent of willing death.

3 Into the night *Read John 13:21–30*

For the third time Jesus is said to be 'troubled in spirit' (cf. 11:33, when Jesus is beside Lazarus' tomb; and 12:27, at the thought of his 'hour'). Knowledge of what lies ahead is no antidote to anxiety. For the first time Jesus speaks openly about his impending betrayal. In the synoptic gospels, the disciples are shocked by Jesus' announcement. Here they are merely 'uncertain of whom he spoke'. In all four gospels we have the impression that Jesus could be talking about any one of them. There is nothing to identify Judas as the obvious candidate for betrayal.

Only here do we come across the disciple 'whom Jesus loved'. His anonymity invites speculation as to his identity, and Lazarus, 'he whom you love' (11:3), is as likely a candidate as anyone. More important than his name is his position, 'lying close to the breast of Jesus' as they reclined at table, and therefore party to 'the quiet disclosures of the Saviour' (Stibbe). Alert readers will compare the beloved disciple's intimacy with Jesus to the Son's intimacy with the Father: 'No one has ever seen God; the only Son, who is in the bosom of the Father, he has made him known' (1:18). The privileged place of intimacy is the source of true revelation—in this case, Jesus' knowledge of his betrayer which the beloved disciple passes on to Simon Peter.

In the synoptics, Jesus leaves it open that any of those at table with him might betray him (see Mark 14:20). Here he dips the morsel into a sauce and gives it to Judas. But still this does not entirely remove the disciples' uncertainty—except, of course, in the case of Judas. 'Satan entered into him.' Only Luke of the other evangelists mentions Satan (see 22:3), though he gives the impression that this diabolical work preceded the supper. The devil's instrument immediately leaves the table and breaks fellowship with Jesus. 'It was night': Judas shows himself to be one who 'loved darkness rather than light, because (his) deeds were evil' (3:19). In the presence of the light of the world, the truth of his actions is exposed (cf. 3:20).

The association of Judas with Satan recalls Jesus' earlier debates with those who are 'of your father the devil … a murderer from the beginning … a liar and the father of lies' (8:44). The conflict that will bring about Jesus' death is not merely a difference of opinion between Jewish teachers, or a necessary sacrifice designed to ward off the unwelcome attention of Rome (11:47ff). It is nothing less than the cosmic struggle between light and darkness, truth and falsehood, good and evil, a struggle in which we all have a stake.

4   Into God's glory   *Read John 13:31–38*

In his commentary on the significance of Jesus' passion, the evangelist interprets it as Jesus' 'departing out of this world to the Father', his 'going to God' (13:1, 3). Here Jesus speaks of 'glory' to refer to this same movement: 'Now is the Son of man glorified and in him God is glorified' (v. 31). 'Glory' has been associated with Jesus' signs since the wedding at Cana (2:11). But the glorification of Jesus himself was first mentioned in 7:39: 'as yet the Spirit had not been given, because Jesus was not yet glorified'. Lazarus' illness was 'for the glory of God, so that the Son of God may be glorified by means of it' (11:4). By precipitating the crucifixion of Jesus (11:47ff), the raising of Lazarus is the sign *par excellence* of his glory. In 12:23 Jesus solemnly announced, 'The hour has come for the Son of man to be glorified': the 'now' of verse 31 gives the unmistakable sense that the whole narrative has been moving towards this moment. The greatest sign, the one that all the others point to, the definitive revelation of God's glory, is imminent.

What is 'now' for Jesus is not so for the disciples: 'Where I am going, you cannot come.' Jesus had bemused and irritated the Jewish leaders with his talk of going away (7:33–34; 8:21). But his intention here in repeating his earlier words is entirely different. Between the 'now' of Jesus and the 'afterward' of the disciples (v. 36) is a task, a mission for which they have been called and chosen. In Moses' final words to Israel, he encouraged them and their children to 'be careful to do all the words of this law. For it is no trifle to you, but it is your life' (Deuteronomy 32:46f). Jesus supplies a 'new commandment … that you love one another, even as I have loved you … By this all men will know that you are my disciples' (vv. 34, 35). As they exemplify the way of Jesus the servant, the disciples are to be the life-giving presence of Jesus in his absence.

Simon Peter wants so much to be 'part' of Jesus, to be where he is, yet he easily overestimates his ability to follow him. He is not yet ready to lay down his life for his Lord, though one day he will (21:18f). As we shall see in the appendix to the gospel (21:15ff) there are lessons to be learned from his coming failure before he can take his place in the mission of Jesus.

5   Going to the Father's house   *Read John 14:1–14*

With chapter 14, Jesus' farewell discourse properly begins. From now on there is a minimum of comment from the evangelist. Jesus speaks uninterrupted except for those occasions when the disciples do not understand. And then, typically, their questions draw out his meaning.

Jesus starts by addressing the anxiety generated by his words, 'Where I am going you cannot come.' This passage's traditional associations with death—it is commonly read to the dying, and used at funeral services—can lead us to interpret 'my Father's house' as heaven, and Jesus' coming 'to take you to myself' as lying beyond a believer's death. But in this gospel, 'my Father's house' is the temple (2:16), and the temple is Jesus' body (2:21). 'The hour is coming, and now is' when communion with God will not require the mediation of a temple, either Jewish or Samaritan: 'true worshippers will worship the Father in spirit and truth' (4:21ff). Living in the Father's house is therefore a metaphor for the communion with God made available by Jesus, notably through his death: 'when I am lifted up from the earth, I will draw all people to myself' (12:32). So Jesus consoles his anxious disciples by promising a share in his own fellowship with the Father, to be realized not after their death, but when 'I will come again and… take you to myself'.

Thomas speaks for those who do not understand Jesus' talk of 'the way' to this communion with the Father. 'I am the way, the truth and the life' is what we would expect from one who claims to be the true revelation of the Father's words and works, and promises a share in his own life-giving relationship with God. Jesus is the revelation of what he promises: heaven and earth meet in the Word made flesh (1:14), the Son of man (1:51), the temple of God (2:16, 21). All this makes sense—doesn't it?

Not to Philip. Jesus' explanation goes beyond the language of representation (cf. 13:20—'he who receives me receives him who sent me'), and speaks of mutual indwelling. Jesus brings about communion with the Father because 'I am in the Father and the Father (is) in me'. This is not some vague mysticism, but Jesus' equality with God (5:18) and unity with the Father (10:30), which lend weight to his absolute 'I am' sayings (8:58). Jesus' antidote to his disciples' anxiety lies in 'knowing' and 'seeing' him. This means believing in him as the Son who lives in the Father and in whom the Father lives; and doing his works—or rather, letting Jesus continue his works in them, through the prayer of asking (vv. 12–14). From Jesus the disciples learn that life-giving faith in him is enough to bring about communion with the One with whom he is in communion.

Or rather, it *will be* enough. There is still the interval between his going away and his 'coming again (to) take you to myself'. For the moment, the disciples must wait. And we must wait to discover what Jesus means by his coming.

6 Coming to the disciples   Read John 14:15–31

In verse 10, Jesus spoke of his relationship with the Father in terms of indwelling: 'I am in the Father and the Father (is) in me.' If the disciples are to enter into Jesus' relationship with the Father and find their home in heaven, they will need to experience a similar indwelling. There are two sides to this. For their part, the disciples are called to reproduce the servant-style love they have seen in Jesus: 'If you love me, you will keep my commandments' (v. 15; cf. vv. 21, 23). But there is also a heavenly side, the dimension of grace, the Father's gift of 'another Counsellor, to be with you for ever'. Notice the parallels between the gift of the Counsellor, the coming of Jesus and his revelation to the disciples (vv. 18, 21), and the indwelling of the Father and the Son in those who live by love (v. 23). Jesus' promise to bring his disciples to his Father's house is fulfilled in the coming of the Counsellor, who allows Father and Son to 'make (their) home' in the disciples (v. 23). On this understanding, then, believers enter heaven, not at Jesus' 'second coming' (as in 1 Thessalonians 4:13ff), or when they die (as in Philippians 1:21ff), but through the gift of the Spirit.

Notice the terminology that is used here for the Holy Spirit. 'Counsellor' translates the Greek *parakletos*, a legal term for one who speaks in defence of another in court. Jesus is referred to in this sense in 1 John 2:1. '*Another* Counsellor' suggests one *of the same kind*: like Jesus, the Counsellor is sent from the Father, and is not received by the world which rejects his teaching (v. 24). Verse 26 suggests that 'the Spirit of truth' means 'the Spirit who communicates the truth about Jesus who is the truth'. 'Holy Spirit' links this passage with the beginning and end of the gospel: the descent of the Spirit at Jesus' baptism, and the Baptist's testimony that Jesus will 'baptize with the Holy Spirit' (1:32, 33); the anticipation of the gift of the Spirit once Jesus has been glorified (7:39; 20:22). Each of these terms, then, connects the promise of Jesus with the Father's gift and the Son's character and mission.

The coming of the Spirit will more than compensate for the disciples' sense of loss and desolation once Jesus has gone. The Spirit will make Jesus present in three ways: first, in the love that characterizes believers (vv. 15, 21, 23); second, by bringing his teaching to life in new situations (v. 26—something of which this gospel is an eloquent example); and third, in his parting gift of peace (vv. 27ff, which pick up the themes of vv. 1–4). 'My peace'—Jesus' gift of communion with God—is a source of consolation and hope. It is 'not as the world gives' because it is present in Jesus even when he is most troubled. So it will sustain the disciples as it sustains him, when they too are threatened by 'the world' and its 'ruler'.

GUIDELINES

The theme of Jesus' presence and absence has threaded through this week's readings. John's eucharistic language in chapter 6 is among the most realistic of its kind in the New Testament. By removing it from the last supper, he makes the point that however important the eucharist may be, the presence of Jesus cannot be confined to it. The living Jesus is known, not simply or even primarily in the breaking of the bread (as in Luke 24:31, 35), but through the common life of his followers—following his example, living by his teaching, and enlivened by the Holy Spirit. The eucharist has an essential part to play in sustaining this shared experience, not least in the way it nourishes the Christian community with the story of the one who gives his flesh for the life of the world, the Bread of Life.

Lord, in the absence of your flesh
remind us of your presence
in acts of service and words of teaching,
through the Bread of Life and the coming of the Spirit.

15–21 MARCH   **JOHN 15:1—17:26**

1   In the vine   *Read John 15:1–17*

'Rise, let us go hence' in 14:31 looks like an ending, but the discourse continues. In the prophets Israel is compared to a vine (Jeremiah 2:21) or a vineyard (Isaiah 5). There is some evidence that this imagery was used of the temple at the time of Jesus. Here he applies it to himself. The *true* vine is analogous to the *good* shepherd: these images can be used of others, but in Jesus they find their definitive form.

The work of the vine dresser—breaking off dead branches and pruning fruitful ones—is essential if the vine is to flourish. Dead branches suggest fruitless disciples. The Greek words for 'prune' and 'make clean' are related, so that the work of pruning is achieved by the cleansing impact of Jesus. There are echoes here of chapter 13, where the disciples are made 'clean' by the foot-washing—except for Judas, who breaks off his fellowship with Jesus and the others.

There are parallels too between *abiding in the vine* here and *living in the house* in chapter 14. There, the disciples love Jesus by keeping his commandments, and live in the Father's house with him; in them live Jesus, the Spirit, and the Father and the Son. Here the disciples abide in Jesus (v. 4) and in his love (v. 9); in them abide Jesus (v. 4) and his words (v. 7). The imagery may be different, but the experience is the same: devotion to Jesus and his way of servant love issues in the richest possible communion with God. Notice that there is nothing passive about this. 'Living' and 'abiding' are associated with a similar expectation of prayer (cf. vv. 7, 8, 16 and 14:13). And prayer promotes mission, by allowing the works of Jesus to continue through his disciples (14:12), and enabling the word of Jesus to bear fruit in them, as it did through the Samaritan woman (see especially 4:39–41, with its reference to Jesus' word and his 'staying'—the same Greek word as 'abiding').

Verses 12–17 gather up much of Jesus' teaching from chapter 13 onwards. Verse 12 repeats 13:34, and verse 13 specifies what Jesus means by 'as I have loved you'. Disciples as 'friends' continues Jesus' subversion of traditional hierarchies (cf 13:14), and defines the nature of his relationship with those who live with him and abide in him. As friends, they have privileged access to revelation (in this sense, the experience of the disciple whom Jesus loved in 13:23ff should not be thought of as unique), but they do not treat this as secret information. 'I chose you and appointed you that you should go and bear fruit and that your fruit should abide.' The vine lives by reproducing itself. Jesus chooses his friends to be the agents of God's continuing mission.

2 Out of the world, out of the synagogues
Read John 15:18—16:4a

The community of Jesus' disciples/friends—living in his Father's house and abiding in the true vine—constitutes the presence of Jesus in his absence: 'he who receives anyone whom I send receives me' (13:20). But if 'his own people received him not' (1:11), his friends dare not expect a better reception: 'a servant is not greater than his master'. 'The world' lives by the principle 'like cleaves to like': it loves its friends and hates its enemies. So Jesus warns his disciples to anticipate a rough ride as they carry out his mission.

Verses 22–24 are a resumé of Jesus' encounters with the Jewish leaders in chapters 5—10. By doing God's life-giving works, he exposed the sin of unbelief among Israel's leaders. In a gospel which uses sight as a metaphor for faith—seeing is believing—seeing *without* believing can only mean one thing: not indifference or agnosticism but hatred. 'He who has seen me has seen the Father' (14:9); and he who has seen-me-but-not-seen-me 'hates me (and) hates my Father also' (v. 23). Tragically, their own law convicts those who 'hated me without a cause' (the words are drawn from Psalm 35:19 and Psalm 69:4): so they have no excuse. Notice how the quotation from 'their law' reverses the positions of accused and accusers. Now it is 'the world', not Jesus, that is under judgment. Inspired by the Counsellor/Spirit of truth, the disciples 'who have been with me from the beginning' will testify on Jesus' behalf.

In 16:1–4a, the narrative leaps beyond its own immediate time frame to 'the hour (that) is coming', when Jesus' disciples will face expulsion from the Jewish community, and even martyrdom. We are in the world of 9:22, when those who confess Jesus as Messiah are thrown out of the synagogue, and the image of the grain of wheat applies (12:24–26). The Johannine community is, not surprisingly, troubled by the absence of Jesus and needs assurance of his presence in the face of the world and its ruler (cf. 14:30). Hence the importance of all that has been said about living and abiding in chapters 14 and 15. 'I have said all this to keep you from falling away'—that is, to enable them to continue in their devotion to Jesus and his servant-style love; to realize the significance of the Father's gift of the Spirit; to live in the peace and joy that are the gifts of Jesus; to hear his word in all that the Spirit teaches them; to let his works bear fruit through prayer, in their mission; and to sustain one another lovingly against the forces that threaten them, as they threatened Jesus. Most of all, they must remember that the world's hatred is not a mark of failure, but of fellowship with the Lord who is also their friend.

3   To the Father—to you   *Read John 16:4b–15*

The rest of chapter 16 repeats much of chapter 14. After a long absence—since 14:22—the disciples reappear, though it is their silence that draws Jesus' comment. Sorrow at the prospect of separation has exorcized their enquiring spirit. Can they grasp that his departure and the coming of the Counsellor will be to their advantage? Not immediately, perhaps, but they will as they come to appreciate his work.

- *'He will prove the world wrong about sin' (NRSV): the coming of the Spirit through the death of Jesus will expose the unbelieving world's error in rejecting him.*

- 'He will prove the world wrong about righteousness': the gift of the Holy Spirit through the shameful death of Jesus will reverse the world's judgment of him. He is the truly righteous person, 'the one on whom you see the Spirit descend and remain' (1:33), not a false prophet who leads the people astray (7:12), or an agent of the devil (8:48), or a sinner (9:24), or a blasphemer (10:33).

- 'He will prove the world wrong about judgment': the coming of the Spirit will vindicate Jesus' claims and his cause, and convict Jesus' enemies on account of their complicity with 'the ruler of this world'.

Verses 12–15 draw together Jesus' earlier teaching about the Holy Spirit from 14:17, 26; 15:26 and 16:7, to emphasize the authority of the Spirit. When the Spirit enables the beleaguered disciples to testify to Jesus, they will not be offering their own opinion or defending their own corner. Like Jesus, they too will be speaking on behalf of God, because the Spirit 'will speak whatever he hears', presumably from the Father who will send him. 'He will take what is mine and declare it to you'—and 'what is mine' comes from the Father. Jesus' promise of the Spirit is intended to reassure the disciples, and renew their confidence. 'He will declare to you the things that are to come', in that his presence will pronounce God's judgment on the world that rejects Jesus (cf. v. 8). And 'he will guide you into all the truth', to deepen the disciples' faith in the one who is 'going to him who sent me'.

4 In sorrow, in joy   Read John 16:16–33

The disciples recover their voice as they talk among themselves about Jesus' enigmatic 'little while'. 'A little while and you will see me no more' corresponds to the earlier 'yet a little while I am with you' (13:33). 'Again a little while and you will see me' picks up 'you shall follow afterward … I shall come again and take you to myself' (13:36, 14:3), with all this entails about the coming of the Spirit. It is important for the disciples to realize that Jesus' departure is an 'hour' and not a single moment. It will bring its share of sorrow; but it will also contain joy.

To get this across, Jesus uses the image of a woman giving birth. Just as her 'hour' is one of sorrow and joy, so the disciples' grief 'in a little while' will turn to joy after 'again a little while', when his glorification will issue in the coming of the Spirit: 'I will see you again and your hearts will rejoice, and no one will take your joy from you' (cf. 15:11). Though his approaching death feels like the end of the world to his disciples, the metaphor of childbirth holds out the prospect of a new beginning. Verse 21 anticipates the scene at the foot of the cross in 19:25–27. There Jesus addresses his mother as 'woman', the same word that he uses in 16:21. The woman giving birth has her 'hour'; the cross is Jesus' 'hour', and also his mother's: 'from that hour the disciple took her to his own home'. Through the suffering of Jesus a new humanity is born, one in which family relationships are redrawn.

Fundamental to this new humanity is a different experience of communion with God. The disciples will be able to speak to the Father directly, rather than relying on Jesus to pray for them, as they have until now. The only proviso is that they do this 'in my name'—that is, out of love for Jesus and the desire to keep his commandments; as branches on the true vine; as friends who believe that Jesus has come from the Father and returned to him. Notice their 'now we know… we believe' once Jesus abandons the 'figure' of the 'little while' and speaks plainly of his descent and ascent. (Verse 28 answers the question about Jesus' origins and destiny that was continually raised during his ministry in Jerusalem, and summarizes the message of this gospel.)

Jesus' 'Do you now believe?' does not so much doubt the disciples' integrity as warn them against underestimating their need for what they will receive in 'yet a little while'. The coming hour will break up their little band, as they desert Jesus in the face of 'tribulation' (this word is often used in contemporary Jewish texts to refer to the upheaval and distress which precede the arrival of the era of salvation). To survive the sorrow brought on by the brutal death of their friend and enter into the joy of God's new world will require all the grace that God will make available to them, nothing less than Jesus' gift of 'peace'.

5   On earth, in heaven—in the hour, beyond it

Read John 17:1–19

As Moses prayed for Israel in Deuteronomy 32:1–3, so Jesus prays for his followers as he prepares to leave them. Though he addresses God throughout with the familiar 'Father', this is an unusual prayer—much of it consists of statements rather than petitions. Although there is no mention of the disciples (except when Jesus prays for them), they and the readers of the gospel are clearly intended to overhear. For this is instruction as much as intercession, and the parallels with chapter 13—notably in the statements about Jesus' hour (v. 1; cf. 13:1), his authority (v. 2; cf. 13:3), his finished work (v. 4; cf. 13:1) and his glorification (v. 5 and throughout the prayer; cf. 13:31–32)—show that the prayer brings Jesus' farewell discourse to a close.

'Where' and 'when' are important questions to ask. Where does the prayer take place? We imagine that Jesus is still at the supper table with his disciples: 'these things I speak in the world' (v. 13). Yet we also hear that 'now I am no more in the world, but they are in the world' (v. 11). Jesus prays as one who is still in the world, but not in the world. When does Jesus offer this prayer? He looks back to his finished work on earth (v. 4), yet it is only as he dies that he cries 'it is finished' (19:30). He speaks of having 'kept them in thy name… (and) guarded them' (v. 12), though we have to wait until they are in the garden for an example of this (18:1–11). The prayer suspends conventional understandings of time and space to span time and eternity, earth and heaven. Jesus prays as the Word made flesh who is on his way to the bosom of the Father (1:14, 18; cf. vv. 5, 24).

The prayer falls into three roughly equal sections—verses 1–8, 9–19, 20–26—each beginning with a reference to Jesus praying. In the first he builds on the disciples' declaration in 16:30—'now we know … we believe'—to express his confidence in them: 'they have kept thy word … they know that everything that thou hast given me is from thee … they know in truth that I came from thee' (vv. 6–8). Yet the second section shows that in the absence of Jesus they need grace if they are to remain faithful to all that he has given them. 'Keep them in thy name… that they may be one, even as we are one' (v. 11) harks back to Jesus' new commandment, and his antidote to the disintegrating pressures on the community of disciples from 'the world' and 'the evil one'.

Here, as elsewhere in the farewell discourses, the community of disciples appear to be living through their own experience of suffering. The prayer brings out their solidarity with Jesus. They share in his mission from God (v. 18), and his reception by the world (v. 14; cf. 15:20; 16:2). If they also share his dedication to the Father (v. 19), those who overhear this prayer can have every confidence that his victory over the world and its ruler is also theirs.

6 Thou in me, I in thee, they in us   Read John 17:20–26

Jesus now turns his attention to a wider group of disciples, 'those who believe in me through their word'—the community that is the 'fruit' of his first disciples' mission (see 15:1ff). The petition 'that they may be one, as we are one' echoes verse 11. The fact that this is repeated and described in a much fuller way in verses 21–23 suggests that the Johannine church is under greater threat from disunity than are Jesus' first followers. The unity of the church is to reflect the unity of Father and Son: not dull uniformity, but a shared sense of purpose and mission. Notice that the church's unity is no mere imitation of the unity of the Father and the Son, but the outcome of communion with the divine: 'The glory which thou hast given me I have given them … I in them and thou in me.' That way the followers of Jesus will be 'perfectly one'.

Such unity is not for ease of administration or the stifling of debate. Its purpose is missionary and revelatory: 'so that the world may believe… (and) know that thou hast sent me and loved them even as thou hast loved me'. In the absence of unity, words and life-giving works are inadequate expressions of God's love for the world, because they convey nothing of the rich communion—with God and among the friends of Jesus—to which all people are called. So Jesus prays that his church may be configured by his own heavenly life—the eternal glory and love which characterize his Father's house, now 'in them' through the coming of the Counsellor.

The Church has not yet managed to present itself to the world as the glory and love of heaven on earth. So Jesus' prayer is offered, not only to the Father but also to those who overhear it in every age, who are invited to receive its instruction and make its intercession their own.

GUIDELINES

It is no surprise when a community that is forced to endure hostility from the outside world gathers strength by putting up barriers and turning inwards. Christian churches have done this down the centuries, in common with other religious groups. This defensiveness is sometimes necessary, and at best it is a strategy for survival. John's Gospel is often said to have a more 'sectarian' feel than the others. Yet, paradoxically, it also contains some of the strongest statements about looking beyond the Christian community, and engaging in mission towards those responsible for hostility.

'God so loved the world that he gave his only Son' (3:16) provides the theological basis for courageous engagement with a threatening environment. Jesus' prayer 'that thou shouldst keep them from the evil one' expresses the hope that his followers will never return the hostility they may have to endure.

Lord, show us the difference
between robust proclamation of the gospel
based on love for the world,
and defensive promotion of our message
for the sake of self-preservation.

22–28 MARCH   **JOHN 18:1—19:42**

---

1 **From the garden to the house of Annas** *Read John 18:1–14*

Chapters 18 and 19 tell of Jesus' arrest, interrogations and execution. The basic outline of events is common to all four gospels, though the details are very different here, as we shall see.

In the synoptics, the garden is named as 'Gethsemane': Jesus prays for strength there before his arrest. Here the garden is unnamed, and is simply a place where Jesus and his disciples regularly meet; so it is known to Judas. Only in this gospel is the betrayer accompanied by Roman soldiers. There is no need for a kiss of identification: Jesus, not Judas, takes the initiative by coming out and identifying himself. It is as if he has gone to the garden to wait for Judas. When the soldiers and officers finally arrive, Jesus as good as invites them to arrest him. His 'I am he' shows that even when he is taken into custody and placed in the hands of his enemies, his divine authority is undiminished. If anything it appears with greater intensity. Those who seize him fall to the ground: they are in the presence of divinity.

There is no question of Jesus' disciples deserting him and fleeing for their lives: he guards them and procures their safety, like the good shepherd who cares for his sheep. So he fulfils the words of his prayer (17:12). Only here is Peter named as the disciple who injures the high priest's slave; and only here is the slave named as Malchus. In Matthew and Luke, Jesus rebukes this violence, and in Luke he goes on to heal the slave's injury. Here he warns Peter against preventing his drinking the cup that his Father has given him.

Only in this gospel is Jesus taken to the house of Annas, the father-in-law of Caiaphas, after his arrest. Annas had been high priest from AD6 to 15, and was succeeded by five sons, as well as his son-in-law Caiaphas. He evidently remained a man of great influence, and it is not improbable that Jesus should appear before him first. But there is no record of any interrogation, simply the reminder of Caiaphas' earlier remarks (11:49f). In their collusion with Judas and the Roman authorities, the Jewish leaders are driven by political expediency. This is but one of the powers at work in the crucifixion, and as we shall see, it is no match for the power of God revealed in the vulnerability of Jesus.

2 Outside and inside the house of Annas *Read John 18:15–27*

The narrative moves backwards and forwards between two scenes: in the courtyard attention focuses on Peter; in the house, on Jesus. The other disciple with Peter only appears in this gospel. His identity is a mystery; his only function for the readers is to explain how it is that Peter managed to gain access to the courtyard.

Whatever else it does, Peter's denial underlines the authority of Jesus, who had announced it in advance at the supper (13:38). Peter's 'I am not' in the courtyard is in sharp contrast to Jesus' 'I am he' in the garden. Annas' questions are general. Perhaps he wants to know how many disciples Jesus has. Are they armed? Do they intend to take Jerusalem by force? As for Jesus' teaching, surely Annas is sufficiently in touch with his own people to know what Jesus has been saying to them. It is, of course, ironic that Jesus should be commending the testimony of those who have heard his teaching to Annas, just as one of his closest disciples is outside, denying all knowledge of him.

Jesus' reply earns him a blow from one of the officers, out to defend Annas' honour. But Jesus stands his ground: the assault is as unnecessary as the line of questioning. Jesus is not charged with any misdemeanour, and Annas makes no attempt at rigorous interrogation. There would be no point: the Jewish leaders have already made up their minds about Jesus (11:47ff), and his elusiveness does nothing to change them.

Peter, meanwhile, is much more forthcoming—a second 'I am not', this time to the servants and officers who made the charcoal fire that keeps him warm. Then a further denial to one of the high priest's slaves, a relative of Malchus and a witness to the events in the garden. (There is no mention here of Peter's accent giving him away.) The cock crows without any reference to Peter's emotional response as he remembers Jesus' words. It is enough to record the denials: they remind us of the urgency of Jesus' prayer for the faithfulness of his disciples in a hostile world (17:14ff).

3 To Caiaphas, then to Pilate *Read John 18:28–38a*

In the synoptic accounts, Caiaphas is the key Jewish interrogator, but not here. John's main interest lies in the confrontation between Jesus and Pontius Pilate, the Roman governor, whose official residence was the praetorium. Again it is ironic that the

Jews who take Jesus to Pilate can be so concerned about contact with a Gentile disqualifying them from eating the Passover, when they are guilty of a much more serious form of defilement: rejection of Jesus as the one sent by God.

The account of Jesus' interrogation by Pilate (18:28—19:16) is carefully constructed. There are seven scenes, with Pilate moving in and out of the praetorium between Jesus and the Jewish leaders. In the first scene (vv. 29–32), Pilate wants to know why Jesus has been brought to him. 'Evildoer' is not specific enough to attract his attention, as his 'take him yourselves and judge him by your own law' implies. But there is more to Pilate's remark than indifference. He is shrewd enough to know what the Jewish leaders want, and ruthless enough to rub salt in their wounds. An occupied people was denied the power of execution; otherwise the Jews would not be petitioning the governor. If Jesus is to be executed, it will be by crucifixion, not stoning. The powerlessness of the Jewish leaders only serves to highlight the authority of their victim (v. 32; cf 12:32).

The second scene (vv. 33–38a) takes Pilate indoors to question Jesus. 'Are you the king of the Jews' is found in all four gospels, but only here is the conversation developed. 'Am I a Jew?' shows Pilate's contempt. He is not really concerned about Jesus or the Jewish nation. He showed no interest in Jesus' kingship until others raised the matter with him. It is left to Jesus to pursue the issue. 'My kingship is not of this world' does not mean that Jesus is an other-worldly figure, indifferent to human affairs (including politics). Jesus makes the point that his kingship is of a different kind, deriving its authority not from human institutions or aspirations—then 'my servants would fight'—but from God.

'So you are a king?' ... 'You say that I am a king.' Pilate uses the right words, but Jesus alters their meaning. Jesus rules by bearing witness to the truth: '(He) ... asserts the claim of God on the world, and his testimony achieves its consummation here before Pilate' (Rensberger, p.97). But such reinterpretation is beyond Pilate. 'What is truth?' is hardly the question of a genuine enquirer. With the embodiment of truth staring him in the face, he goes outside to play games with the Jews once more.

The third scene (vv. 38b–40) has Pilate calling the Jewish leaders' judgment into question, and taunting them: 'I find no crime in him … will you have me release for you the king of the Jews?' There is no known evidence of the custom of releasing a prisoner at the festival, but it fits in with the central theme of the Passover celebration. It is ironic that the Jewish leaders (not the crowds, as in the synoptic accounts) should ask for Barabbas' release. In this gospel he is a 'robber': the term was applied to those who resorted to violence to escape the hardship brought on by Roman rule in Palestine. No doubt some sections of society would sympathize with him—but the Jewish leaders? As a 'robber' he reminds us of those who climb into the sheepfold another way (10:1), the antithesis of the good shepherd. That the Jewish leaders should prefer a man of violence to Jesus is a sad comment on their morality.

The fourth scene (vv. 1–3) appears to make nonsense of Pilate's belief in Jesus' innocence. Is he buckling under pressure from the Jews? Rensberger thinks not. Pilate uses the scourging and mockery of Jesus to ridicule Jewish nationalism. Unlike in the synoptic versions, the governor presents Jesus to the Jews as a mock king in the fifth scene (vv. 4–8). He finds no guilt, no threat, in Jesus: 'Behold the man'—this "ludicrous figure, in whom he portrays just how preposterous he finds the idea of a Jewish 'king'". In this "bitter burlesque of Jewish royalty" (Rensberger), not only Jesus but also the leaders of his people are humiliated. Pilate has still more contempt to offer: 'Take him yourselves and crucify him.' They can't, of course, because they have been deprived of their authority over their own nation (18:31).

Sensing, perhaps, that their desires are about to be frustrated, the Jews protest that Jesus is not as innocent as he appears. Under their law, he is guilty of blasphemy because 'he has made himself the Son of God'. Only in this gospel is this charge brought before Pilate, who becomes 'very much afraid' (a better translation than the RSV's 'more afraid', because he has shown no fear up to now). He returns indoors to Jesus for the sixth scene (vv. 9–11). Pilate's 'Where are you from?' picks up the debates raging throughout Jesus' Jerusalem ministry (7:27–28; 9:29–30). Jesus' silence brings out the point he made then to those who judge by worldly criteria: 'You do not know where I come from or where I am going' (8:14, NRSV). When Pilate tries to assert his authority over Jesus, he is told that it is not Rome but God ('from above') who allows him his power, and then only to fulfil God's purpose by using the world's unbelief and hatred to glorify Jesus. Rome is effectively powerless; its governor acts out of ignorance—which is why the 'greater sin' lies with the Jewish leaders.

In the seventh and final scene (vv. 12–16), Pilate tries seriously for the first time to have Jesus released. But he is stopped in his tracks as the Jews pick up the political baton once more by playing on his loyalty to Caesar. This only aggravates Pilate's callousness and contempt. He brings Jesus out to them (it is not clear whether Jesus or Pilate sits on the judgment seat) and bullies them into abandoning their nationalist hopes by confessing their loyalty to the Emperor. 'We have no king but Caesar' jars with the sentiments of the Passover hymns that celebrate the sole sovereignty of *God* over Israel. Israel's leaders are paying a high price to preserve their place in the power structures by having Jesus crucified. In the evangelist's eyes it is they, not Jesus, who are the real blasphemers.

5 To Golgotha *Read John 19:17–37*

Like the other evangelists, John does not detail the crucifixion itself. His account contains a number of unique features. Jesus carries his own cross. The inscription which bears his 'crime' is written in three languages. On the cross he is not mocked, either by the spectators or those crucified either side of him. Four women stand close to the cross, corresponding to four soldiers, along with the beloved disciple, whose eye-witness testimony lies behind John's account. There is no darkness over the land, no tearing of the temple curtain, no cry of god-forsakenness just before Jesus dies. The soldiers only cast lots for his seamless tunic. He speaks to his mother and the beloved disciple standing by. He fulfils scripture consciously: there is no wine mixed with myrrh to dull his pain; the sponge of vinegar on the stalk of

111

hyssop (a small wall-growing plant) is to quench his thirst. He seems to choose his moment of death, and his last words testify to the completion of his work. There is no need to break his legs to help him die, though a soldier stabs his side with a spear.

The evangelist uses these details to bring out his understanding of the meaning of Jesus' death. He needs no help to complete his work on the cross, and his undiminished sovereignty is universal, however ironic Pilate's insistence on this may be. His tunic symbolizes the one flock he creates by laying down his life (10:15–16; cf. 17:11, 21). His mother's needs take priority over his own pain, as a new community is born through his passion. Hyssop (which is used in the Passover ceremonies) and unbroken legs testify to the death of the unblemished Passover Lamb of God (Exodus 12:46; cf. 1:29. In 19:14 he is condemned at the sixth hour, ie midday, on the day of Preparation, just as the Passover lambs are being slaughtered). Whatever their medical significance, blood and water are signs of the life made available to the world through the exaltation of Jesus (cf. 6:63, 4:10, 3:14f).

We should not lose sight of the political significance of Jesus' death. 'King of the Jews' takes up Israel's hopes for freedom and a new world, but transcends them. 'If the Son makes you free, you will be free indeed' (8:36). This is liberation from the self-absorption of sin into the service of Israel's true king, whom Jesus calls 'Father'. Pilate and the Jewish leaders are one in representing those who serve 'the ruler of this world', preferring 'the father of lies' to the truth. Their politics, fed by violence and compromise, can only spell death, not life.

'It is finished.' In one sense there is nothing more to say. Jesus' crucifixion is the hallmark of his faithfulness to the one who sent him; the extent of his love for his own; his victory over the world and its death-dealing ways; and the supreme revelation of the redeeming love that lies at the heart of creation.

6   From the cross to the tomb   *Read John 19:38–42*

Joseph of Arimathea and Nicodemus bring echoes of earlier parts of the gospel. Joseph is a 'secret disciple', more concerned to preserve his honour in the Jewish community than to confess his faith in Jesus openly (cf. 9:22; 12:42f). Nicodemus, who only appears in this gospel, had previously warned the Jewish ruling council not to condemn Jesus without a hearing (7:50f), though to no avail. These two men are courageous in approaching the cynical and manipulative Pilate. They are genuinely concerned that the Passover celebrations should not be marred by the shame of an unburied Jewish body. With their 'hundred pounds of myrrh and aloes' (an extravagant quantity) they give Jesus 'a burial fit for the king of kings' (Stibbe). Notice the differences between John's account and the synoptics. They have Jesus' body wrapped in a linen shroud, to be embalmed after the sabbath. Here linen cloths are used, reminders of the raising of Lazarus in 11:44.

What are we to make of Joseph's and Nicodemus' actions here? Some see this as open devotion, an act of faith in Jesus. But the reference to Nicodemus' earlier visit to Jesus 'by night' (3:2) suggests a different perspective. For all their bravery, piety and generosity, the men make no confession of faith in Jesus. Indeed 'Nicodemus shows himself capable only of burying Jesus, ponderously and with a kind of absurd finality, so loading him down with burial as to make it clear that he does not expect a resurrection any more than he expects a second birth' (Rensberger). Is this too harsh a judgment on them?

What we can certainly say is that these two honourable Jewish men prepare John's readers for a resurrection of a wholly different order from that of Lazarus, not least by providing the perfect foil for the first witness to Easter faith, Mary Magdalene.

GUIDELINES

The great classical writer Ovid completed his epic poem *Metamorphoses*, which retells the great myths of the ancient world, around the time of the birth of Christ, when the emperor Augustus ruled. In the introduction to his *Tales from Ovid* (Faber and Faber, 1997), Ted Hughes writes of Ovid's world: 'For all its Augustan stability, it was at sea in hysteria and despair, at one extreme wallowing in the bottomless appetites and sufferings of the gladiatorial arena, and at the other searching higher and higher for a spiritual transcendence—which eventually did take form, on the crucifix.'

That the crucifixion of Jesus should meet the deepest spiritual needs of human beings, then and now, is as much a surprise as a mystery. At one level, it is an example of the very worst that human beings do to one another. Yet this gospel would have us 'see' it at another level—as the presence of God, in love and judgment; and as the power of love, lifting the world beyond hostility into an all-embracing communion.

Lord, as we survey your wondrous cross,
guard us from doing anything to extend its tragedy,
and renew our faith and hope
through the vision of love so amazing, so divine.

---

29 MARCH–4 APRIL   JOHN 20:1—21:25

1 To the tomb, early   *Read John 20:1–10*

All four gospels tell of a visit to Jesus' tomb by a woman or women (in the synoptics the women had seen where Jesus was buried and so could identify the tomb) early on the day after the sabbath, some thirty-six hours or so after Jesus' burial. The stone sealing the entrance to the tomb is rolled back, and the body gone. In or around the tomb are one or more angels. But there the similarities end. Only here does Mary Magdalene go to the tomb alone, and after seeing it open report the news to Simon Peter and the beloved disciple. Her first thought is that the body has been removed by Jesus' enemies, or perhaps grave robbers, and dumped elsewhere.

John alone has the two men dashing to the tomb (in Luke 24:12 Peter goes; this verse is not found in all manuscripts, and is probably a later addition, based on John 20:3–10). Unlike Mary, they go in—Peter, the slower runner, first—and see the grave clothes, but no body. What do they make of this? The beloved disciple 'saw and believed'. What did they believe? That Jesus had been raised from the dead? Hardly: 'for as yet they did not know the scripture that he must rise from the dead'. When he saw that the body was missing, the beloved disciple believed Mary's report that the grave had been tampered with and the body removed.

Several scholars offer a different reading of the beloved disciple's response, for two reasons. First, if the beloved disciple is Lazarus, the sight of the grave clothes would remind him of his own experience (the Greek word for 'napkin' in verse 7 is the same as that translated by 'cloth' in 11:44). Second, verse 29 uses 'seeing' and 'believing' to refer to Thomas' faith in the resurrection of Jesus. So, it is argued, when the beloved disciple *sees* the missing body and the neatly-placed grave clothes, he *believes* that Jesus has been raised from the dead.

There are difficulties, however, with this interpretation. Why does the evangelist need to mention the disciples' ignorance of the scripture in verse 9 if they do not need it in order to make sense of what they 'see'? (It is not clear which biblical text the evangelist is referring to: perhaps it is the general testimony of scripture, as in 1 Corinthians 15:4, or Psalm 16:8ff, which is used as a proof-text in Acts 2:25ff.) And if they 'see and believe' that Jesus is alive, why do they leave Mary behind, shocked and grieving?

These problems are resolved once we realize that *what* the beloved disciple sees and *what* Thomas sees are different. The beloved disciple sees grave clothes in an otherwise empty tomb, but Thomas sees Jesus alive over a week after his execution. This allows him to accept for himself the testimony of the other (male) disciples, and of Mary. A tomb from which Jesus' body is missing is not sufficient evidence for the resurrection of Jesus from the dead. It is at best an ambiguous sign, which needs further support from the scriptures, and from what is about to happen to Mary as she stands weeping by the tomb.

2   Beside the tomb   *Read John 20:11–18*

When Mary eventually looks into the tomb, she sees 'two angels in white', sitting as if to emphasize the absence of Jesus' body. Unlike their counterparts in the synoptic accounts, they have no message for Mary about the resurrection of Jesus, only a question: 'Why are you weeping?' Her reply repeats her earlier statement to the men, and reveals the depth of her plight. It is bad enough that her Lord has been executed and his grave violated. But the fact that his body is missing only intensifies her sorrow by highlighting the hopelessness of her state. As those with loved ones who are 'missing, presumed dead' know only too well, the absence of a body imprisons mourners in their grief. It is entirely right that Mary should want to find the body of Jesus.

The resurrection of the dead is the last thing Mary expects. Her failure to recognize the figure she sees behind her in the garden is also understandable on psychological grounds. Non-recognition is a theme found in other Easter stories. The two disciples on the road to Emmaus do not recognize the man who joins them (Luke 24:13ff), and the disciples fishing on the lake do not know who the man on the shore is (John 21:4). Is this because Jesus' appearance has been changed by the resurrection? Or does Mary fail to recognize him because the last time she saw him, his life had been drained out of him by the brutality of crucifixion? Here, as in Luke 24:30f, recognition is triggered by familiarity. The good shepherd calls Mary by name: 'I know my own and my own know me' (10:3, 14) Calls by name/recognising the voice)

The 'little while' between not seeing and seeing Jesus is over (16:16), but his 'do not hold me' implies that relationships are now of a different order. 'I have not yet ascended to my Father' suggests that Jesus' 'lifting up' is a process rather than a single event, an 'hour' rather than an instant. (John has resurrection appearances but, unlike Luke, no moment of ascension.) Jesus, not the angels, gives Mary a message for the other disciples, now called 'brethren': 'I am ascending to my Father and your Father, to my God and your God' is entirely consistent with the talk of 'going to God' in the supper discourses, and the promise of sharing his communion with the Father.

Mary becomes the first evangelist of Easter, and John once again contrasts the testimony of a woman with the inadequate faith of Nicodemus (19:39; cf. the Samaritan woman in chapter 4). Unlike the beloved disciple in verse 8, Mary's 'seeing' is believing in the truly Johannine sense, and her statement shows the significance for Easter faith of the sight of the living Jesus by

First to Mary - Preoccupied all Passover to being at the tomb
— more annointing with oil + tears of love. Even John the beloved is not at the tomb before Mary + Jesus does not appear til after Peter + John have gone!

one who had seen him crucified and buried. It also makes it clear that on its own, the empty tomb is no basis for Easter faith: for this we rely on a woman's witness to the appearance of the living Lord.

3   Behind closed doors   *Read John 20:19–29*

The time references in this passage are significant: 'on the evening of that day... eight days later' suggests a weekly gathering of Jesus' followers on the first day of the week. 'Fear of the Jews' is understandable in the immediate aftermath of the discovery of the empty tomb. Perhaps the disciples will be implicated, and dragged before the authorities. But this early fear resonates with the experiences of John's audience, for whom hostility from 'the world' is a fact of life. We can well imagine their meeting for their weekly celebrations of the resurrection behind closed doors. But these are no barrier to the presence of the living Lord, whose appearance confirms Mary's testimony. He greets the disciples and identifies himself by his wounds. In view of what he had said in the farewell discourses, 'peace be with you' is more than a formal greeting. It addresses hearts that are troubled and afraid (14:1, 27ff), and brings great joy (15:11; 16:20f). As the breath/Spirit of God gave life to the creature he formed from the dust (Genesis 2:7) and the nation rendered lifeless in exile (Ezekiel 37), so Jesus' breathing of the Holy Spirit on the disciples inspires a new creation, and fulfils the promises he made before his death.

Jesus' peace is not therapy for anxiety but the basis of mission, as a frightened band of followers meeting behind closed doors is sent out into a hostile world. Verse 23 summarizes the substance of their mission in terms of the forgiveness and retention of sins. There are parallels with Jesus' words about binding and loosing in Matthew 16:19 and 18:18. In this gospel, however, sin is connected with unbelief. The disciples are charged with bringing forgiveness by opening the eyes of faith in Jesus as the one sent by God. As 16:8ff shows, this is more than a task of apologetics and explanation. It also involves the courage to speak God's word of judgment to a world absorbed in itself.

On this occasion the absent body belongs to Thomas, who resolutely refuses to trust the others' 'we have seen the Lord' (notice how the male disciples have now made Mary's witness their own). His insistence on having the same opportunity to see and touch is rewarded 'eight days later', when, as before, Jesus appears and greets his disciples. Now Thomas too can believe, and on his lips we find the faith of the Johannine church: 'My Lord and my God!' Thomas speaks for those who 'see' the glory of God in the crucified Jesus who has been 'lifted up' to his Father's 'house'. Jesus' closing beatitude is a reminder that the vast majority of Christians believe without seeing. Indeed believing *is* 'seeing', and this is only ever made possible by taking on trust the testimony that has its roots in the witness of Jesus' sisters and brothers.

4 By the sea of Tiberias *Read John 20:30—21:8*

The last two verses of chapter 20 look like an ending. Many scholars think that they concluded an earlier version of the gospel, with chapter 21 as an appendix. Verse 31 has led to debate about the purpose of John's gospel. 'That you may believe… and have life' could suggest that the gospel is an evangelistic work, designed to open the eyes of unbelievers to Jesus as 'the Christ, the Son of God'. But as we have seen, it contains a lot of material that appears to relate to the particular concerns of the Johannine church, notably the importance of bearing confident and faithful witness to Jesus in the face of hostility and the threat of violence. On this understanding, 'that you may believe' carries the sense of *continuing* in the Christian faith: the Greek can be rendered 'that you may go on believing'. The gospel is intended to encourage the church to see itself rightly: to realize that, by virtue of the gift of the Spirit, it represents Jesus in the world: 'as the Father has sent me, so I have sent you.' If servant-style love, life-giving works and faithful witness to Jesus are marks of authenticity, then so too is the world's hostility.

After such an inspiring ending, why the need for an appendix? There are rumours to be corrected about the beloved disciple (vv. 20–23). And there is an important omission to be rectified. The body of the gospel says nothing of any encounter between the living Jesus and Peter. We are not told how he responded to the empty tomb, or the appearance of Jesus among the company of disciples. The singling out of Peter in Mark 16:7—'tell his disciples *and Peter* that he is going before you to Galilee; there you will see him, as he told you'—is significant in view of Peter's threefold denial. The appendix contains the story of their meeting. Whether or not it was written by the author of the gospel, it certainly adopts its style.

What lies behind Peter's 'I am going fishing'? It may be nothing more than the need to earn a living. Even after Easter, Peter and the others cannot support their families on fresh air! It is worth holding on to the sheer ordinariness of this. In the previous chapter, the living Lord appears to Mary in the face of acute pastoral needs, and to the other disciples in what to readers might look like a religious meeting. In the appendix we see that the living Jesus cannot be restricted to pastoral or ecclesiastical settings. He is no stranger to those who are absorbed in the daily routine of earning a living. In these mundane situations it is often difficult to recognize Jesus. Along with Peter, we too might need the help of those like the beloved disciple whose Christian wisdom has made them particularly sensitive to the presence of God. It is worth asking ourselves whether the Bible, prayer and worship, and Christian fellowship are enlarging our view of reality, so that it is as natural for us to picture the presence of the living Lord in the ordinary circumstances of life as it is to imagine fish in the sea.

5   By the fireside   *Read John 21:9–19*

There are parallels between the story of the night's fishing on the sea of Tiberias and the account of Peter's call in Luke 5:1–11. On both occasions, Peter and his companions catch nothing; Jesus tells them to try again, and they manage to land an enormous catch; and Jesus makes a particular point of talking with Peter. Luke and John may be giving different versions of the same incident. What is important here is the setting John gives it. He links it with the feeding of the five thousand in 6:1–15. This too occurs by the sea of Tiberias. In both stories there is a meal of bread and fish, and Jesus' actions with the bread and fish are almost identical. There are clear connections with the passion and Easter narratives. The charcoal fire reminds us of the fire in the high priest's courtyard (18:18—only this gospel refers to it as a charcoal fire). And verses 1 ('after this') and 14 refer back to the events of chapter 20.

The symbolism is of a piece with themes from the gospel. The disciples on the lake are like the sheep who recognize the good shepherd's voice (10:4, 16). The size of their catch reminds us of the fruitfulness of the vine when the words of Jesus abide in the branches (15:7, 8). The unbroken net is an image of the unity of the church, which the good shepherd calls together (10:16) and Jesus prays for (17:11, 20f). And the breakfast is like the eucharist (6:11, 41ff). But no one knows the significance of 153 fish!

It is easy to lose the message of the story among all these connections and symbols. The early morning charcoal fire and the post-breakfast conversation take us to its heart. Three questions in which the good shepherd calls Peter by name—the one he used when he first called him to discipleship in 1:41f, 'Simon son of John'; three enquiries into his loyalty; three positive declarations to undo three denials by another early morning charcoal fire; a threefold recall to the good shepherd's service. Notice that Peter is 'grieved' at Jesus' third question (v. 17). The interrogation has clearly done its work, as Peter's shame surfaces, ready to be healed. Jesus has no intention of allowing him to stay with his past. Healing lies in following, in taking up his discipleship once more. And following will bring him to share his master's glory. 'If anyone serves me, he must follow me; and where I am, there shall my servant be also; if anyone serves me, my Father will honour him' (12:26).

6 Turning and returning *Read John 21:20–25*

Attention now shifts from Peter to the beloved disciple, as the appendix takes up a matter of concern in the Johannine church. Again there are explicit connections with the main body of the gospel (v. 20). Peter's preoccupation with the destiny of another disciple is understandable in view of the seriousness of Jesus' words to him in verse 18. It is as if by turning his head he wants to deflect Jesus' hard sayings from himself on to another. 'If this is what loyal discipleship will bring for *me*, what will it mean for *him*?'

Jesus leaves himself wide open to misunderstanding. He wants Peter to take to heart what he is calling *him* to do and to become. So he asks him to suppose the complete opposite for the other disciple. What if the beloved disciple were to survive to the end of the world, when Jesus comes? What business is that of Peter, the future martyr? (Notice that this is the only example of the idea of the 'second coming' in this gospel. Sayings which express this from the synoptic tradition are paralleled in this gospel by references to the coming of Jesus in the Spirit. Compare 14:3, 18, 23 and Matthew 24:30f.) Despite the fact that the weight of Jesus' words lies not with 'he will remain until I come' but 'what is that to you?', they evidently gave rise to a rumour that the beloved disciple *would* in fact live until then. This is all the more understandable if the beloved disciple was Lazarus, whom Jesus raised from the dead. Those who spread the rumour were guilty of confusing supposition with promise, sign (the raising of Lazarus) with substance (the resurrection of Jesus). They were promoting misunderstanding by spreading misinformation. Verse 24 ascribes a modest, though significant, role to the beloved disciple. He is the author of the written source behind the appendix ('these things' refers to chapter 21 rather than the gospel as a whole). 'We know' (the author of the appendix, writing perhaps on behalf of the leaders of the Johannine church) that his testimony is reliable enough to put an end to speculation, which was presumably interfering with discipleship and mission.

Verse 25 does not match the elegance and power of the original ending in 20:30–31. It is a rather wistful overstatement, but it does remind us that there is more to be said about Jesus than is found in this gospel, or for that matter in any of the others. This in itself ought to inspire modesty, as well as confidence, in those who use this work to nourish their faith in Jesus Christ, the Son of God.

Hopefully we reach the end of the gospel armed with new insights and wanting to reread it in the light of what we now see. This has certainly been my experience in writing these notes. I am left with the impression that the gospel is rather like some of its characters and themes: it is a witness to Jesus Christ, and a sign of his glory. When we benefit from our reading, it is because we absorb into ourselves something of what we have read: the story, the poem becomes part of us. When we read, and reread, this gospel, we may hope to absorb something of its nature as a witness and a sign. What might it mean for us and for the church today to be a witness to Jesus Christ and a sign of his glory?

Help us, Lord, to see your glory through this gospel.
Use our reading
to renew our faith in the Word made flesh,
and to strengthen our witness to the crucified and living Lord.

Further reading

Kenneth Grayston, *The Gospel of John*, Epworth Press 1990, is an accessible and reasonably-priced commentary on the English text.

C.K. Barrett, *The Gospel According to St John*, Second Edition, SPCK 1978, is a richly rewarding commentary on the Greek text.

Mark Stibbe, *John. Readings: A New Biblical Commentary*, JSOT Press 1993, sheds fresh light on the gospel by treating it as a work of literature.

David Rensberger, *Overcoming The World. Politics and Community in the Gospel of John*, SPCK 1988, is a readable collection of essays with insights into the religious and political setting of the gospel.

The Song of Songs

The Song of Songs is unlike any other book in the Bible. Some readers will read it as an anthology of love poetry and welcome its uninhibited celebration of human love. Others will read it as an allegory of God's love for us and ours for him.

We do not know who wrote these poems, who produced the anthology or how it came to be included in Judaism's holy scriptures. We do know that there was some dispute about its status, possibly on the grounds that it did not contain the Divine Name. Rabbi Akiba (who died in AD135) insisted on its holiness, was adamant that it was not a collection of love lyrics and protested against its songs being sung in public houses. He said that the whole world was not worth the day when this song of God's love for Israel was given to his people. And that is the way it is still read in the synagogue at Passover. The Church Fathers took the same allegorical line and read it as a song of God's love for the Church or for each human soul.

I therefore offer you a choice: to read the Song as a book of ancient love poetry or to follow tradition and read it as a celebration of God's love. I divide each section into three. Part (a) explains some of the difficulties in the reading. Part (b) treats the reading literally as a love poem and part (c) treats it as an allegory. Those who find its explicit sexuality too much can miss (b) and those who are not enamoured of allegorical readings can miss (c). In this way I hope that everyone may find something of value in this strange, difficult and beautiful book.

Whichever way we read it, the Song is not an easy read. Hebrew poetry is harder to follow than traditional western poetry or Hebrew prose, and in the Song it is often unclear where individual poems begin and end, or who is speaking. The poems abound in vivid metaphors and rich allusions to places and customs, flora and fauna, perfumes, colours, fashions and jewellery, and the meanings of many of these are lost to us. Often the Hebrew is 'obscure' as well. These difficulties lie behind many of those differences, too numerous to mention, between the various modern translations.

The version used for these notes is the Revised English Bible (REB), which divides the poems between three speakers: Bride, Bridegroom and a chorus of Companions (the 'Daughters of Jerusalem'—see note on 3:5). Some other translations do the same but do not always agree on who says what.

5–11 APRIL   THE SONG OF SONGS 1:1—4:14

---

1   Sweeter than wine   *Read Song of Songs 1:1–8*

(a) 'Song of Songs' means 'The best song' or 'The most beautiful of songs' (GNB). The Good News Bible also notes that the book may be 'by Solomon', 'dedicated to Solomon' or 'for Solomon'. Few scholars think that Solomon wrote it, largely because much of its language is too late for his time. Attributing new books to old heroes was common, and, as the epitome of wisdom (1 Kings 3:3–14, 4:29–34), Solomon's name was attached to Proverbs and Ecclesiastes. Perhaps this song was attributed to him because of his reputation as a great, though unwise, lover (1 Kings 11:1–13).

   The speakers are Bride (vv. 2–4a, 5–7), Bridegroom (v. 8) and the Companions who sing to them both, rejoicing for her and repeating her praise of his love (v. 4b).

   Verse 6 shows that the 'dark and lovely' Bride is embarrassed by her sunburned complexion and needs to explain it, though her explanation is not very clear. Like Cinderella, she is put down and put upon; but she knows that her lover will transform everything for her (v. 7). *Kedar* and *Shalmah* (*Solomon* in some translations) were bedouin tribes. The Bride follows her royal metaphor in verse 4 with a rural one. Her lover is the shepherd and she wants to find him, rather than be left passing the time with the other shepherdesses de-lousing her clothes. Other translations of verse 7b are equally problematic, though less earthy.

(b) The Bride offers herself to her future husband and addresses him as her 'king' (v. 4a). There are parallels in Egyptian and Syrian love poetry for this, as there are widely for the rural idyll of the shepherd and his lass. She yearns for his kisses (v. 2) and company (v. 4a). She flatters him, boasts of her good fortune in securing him against the competition (v. 3) and teases him that she does not know where he is (v. 7).

(c) According to the ancient Jewish commentaries, the Song tells of God's love to Israel and abounds in references to Old Testament incidents and characters. The kisses of verse 2, for example, refer to God's gift of the Law to Moses. Charles Wesley is indebted to the Greek translation of these verses for, 'Jesu, lover of my soul, let me to Thy bosom fly'.

2 Shall I compare thee? *Read Song of Songs 1:9—2:7*

(a) The lovers exchange compliments: Bridegroom (1:9–10), Bride (vv. 12–14), Bridegroom (v. 15), Bride (v. 16a), Bridegroom (vv. 16b–17), Bride (2:1), Bridegroom (v. 2) and Bride (vv. 3–6). The Companions interrupt with encouragement (v. 11). The poem ends with the Bridegroom's enigmatic word to them (v. 7, also 8:4; see note on 3:5).

Song of Songs 1:9–10 is the first of several 'descriptions' in which each tells the other how attractive they are, although not every woman would consider it a compliment to be compared with a royal chariot horse. The now proverbial 'rose of Sharon' was a crocus (see Isaiah 35:1, RSV, NIV) which grew abundantly in Sharon, the inland part of the coastal plain. The lily is a common wild flower, probably red (see 5:13), and not the plant we know by that name. Whether this 'apple tree' and its fruit are related to modern apples is another open question (NEB has 'apricots'). The perfumes and fruits here were almost certainly thought to have aphrodisiac qualities.

(b) Bathed and perfumed, the lovers lie in each other's arms whispering endearments (1:12—2:6). On the whole, Christianity has been suspicious of pleasure in general and sex in particular. By contrast, Judaism tends to insist that life, food and sex are good. The Old Testament is, of course, well aware of the downside of these good things and roundly condemns their abuse. This lovers' dialogue, full of anticipation, excitement and then fulfilment, is a powerful statement of the beauty, joy and mutuality of physical love.

125

(c) We know about loving our neighbour and one another, but Christians find it very easy to overlook that part of the commandment which talks about loving *yourself*. We are brought up to see ourselves as sinners and much of our worship reminds us that that is what we are. In 1:8–10 and 1:15 the Bridegroom keeps on telling his beloved how beautiful she is. In these words, Bernard of Clairvaux (1091–1153), who preached prolifically on this book, heard God telling us how beautiful we are in his sight. May God give us ears to hear what he wrote, so that we too can sing:

> *But what to those who find? Ah! this*
> *Nor tongue nor pen can show:*
> *The love of Jesus, what it is*
> *None but his loved ones know.*

3   A season for love   *Read Song of Songs 2:8–17*

(a) This poem divides between Bride (vv. 8–13), Bridegroom (v. 14), Companions (v. 15) and Bride (vv. 16–17). The Bride rejoices that her Bridegroom is back. The month of May is here (as can be deduced from verses 11–13) and as nature blossoms, so does love. Her lover has come and waits for her to go away with him. Verse 17 might mean that he has come at dawn and the new day is theirs, or that it is now evening and the night is theirs.

We have no idea what verse 15 means. The animals are foxes rather than REB's 'jackals' and they were widely regarded as vermin in the ancient Near East.

(b) The Bridegroom twice calls on his 'darling' to 'rise up' and 'come away' (vv. 10 and 13). Here is that love which needs no one and nothing but itself, climaxing in verse 16a.

Are the Companions reminding us in verse 15 that the course of true love doesn't always run smooth, not least because there are always those who want to spoil the happiness of others?

(c) At the heart of the Bible are an experience and a conviction that God is love (Exodus 34:6–9 and its numerous echoes and 1 John 4:7–12). This is expressed in the Old Testament in the covenant God makes with Israel, in which he commits himself to them as their God and they commit themselves to him as his

126

people (Hosea 2:23). One New Testament expression of this is to picture the Church as the Bride of Christ (Ephesians 5:25ff, Revelation 21:2). Verse 16a is frequently quoted by the rabbis and the Church Fathers to illustrate this love of God to us and our love to him. *Gen " in the cool of the evening"*

Allegorical interpretations of verse 15 are legion. The 'little foxes' who spoil God's vineyard have been seen as anything from the little nations surrounding Israel to those who try to change the rules of a monastery. As one commentator puts it, 'The Church has never lacked foxy foes, within and without, to spoil the vineyard and to whom this verse could be applied.'

4 Night after night   *Read Song of Songs 3:1–5*

(a) Verse 1 is the beginning of a new speech by the Bride. The chorus of Companions, which the Song itself calls the 'Maidens (or Daughters) of Jerusalem', has spoken three times (1:4b, 2:11, 2:15). In verse 5 (which repeats 2:7 and is found again in 8:4) the Bridegroom speaks directly to them (REB and NJB; in NIV it is the Bride who says these lines). What he says is full of problems. He adjures them either not to push them along too quickly or possibly to leave them alone. He swears by the 'hinds and gazelles of the fields'. This oath, which might have links with pagan fertility cults, could be referring to the sexual potency which these animals proverbially had. Or these two words may be substitutions for titles of God to which they are very similar and so may be an example of the tendency to avoid using names for God in secular settings. REB follows the Greek which speaks of the 'powers and forces of the fields' but goes too far when it names them as 'the spirits and goddesses of the field'.

(b) Note the change in tone. So far, every poem has been rapturous; but now we meet our first hint of love's pain. Either the Bride lies in bed waiting for the Bridegroom, who does not come, or she yearns for his presence in her dreams every night. Also, the whole world may *not* love a lover. The city police of verse 3 will reappear with much less patience in 5:7.

(c) Some early Christian writers saw this as a poem about seeking and not finding. One commentator on verse 1 writes, 'As applied to the individual soul... it was taken to indicate the impossibility of finding Christ while reclining in carnal pleasures and in the darkness of sin. Those who seek Christ the easy way do not find him...' Others have seen it as about seeking and finding. The Venerable Bede related verses 1–4 to Mary Magdalene. She looked for her Lord in the night after his crucifixion, came to the tomb with spices, met angels there and asked them about him. Then she found him and tried to hold him. Finally she took the good news of his resurrection back to the room where the disciples were.

5 Who is this? *Read Song of Songs 3:6–11*

(a) These are verses sung to welcome the Bridegroom, though the singer varies in the different modern versions. They are sung by the Companions in REB, by the Bride in NIV and by the narrator-poet in NJB (New Jerusalem Bible). The Bridegroom is pictured as King Solomon making his royal entry into Jerusalem, though there are also clear overtones of the 'pillar of smoke by day and the fire by night' of God's triumphant progress through the wilderness (Exodus 13:21–22). Here the metaphor of the Bridegroom or lover as king, which was hinted at in 1:4 and 1:12, is given full play. His wedding day is the day when he is crowned with joy (v. 11). These verses are a clear allusion to the custom of crowning brides and grooms which ceased when the temple was destroyed in AD70. The role of the groom's mother in the process is unique to this poem, though Solomon himself did owe his throne to his mother, Bathsheba (1 Kings 1:15–31). The 'terrors of the night' in verse 8 is a telling phrase and even for desert caravans these terrors would not have sprung only from the threat of thieves and robbers.

(b) One modern commentator describes this poem as a 'lovers' fantasy' and a 'romantic pipe dream' in which one rich image is piled on another. On the lips of the Companions it is a celebration of marriage in which no pictures, however exaggerated, are quite adequate to describe its importance and how it makes the couple feel.

(c) Jewish tradition delights in seeing the exodus here. Following the pillar of cloud and fire, the people of Israel are coming out of the wilderness and entering the promised land, carrying with them the memory of Abraham in the myrrh, Isaac in the frankincense and Jacob in the powdered spices.

Some of the Church Fathers see here a picture of the soul of a Christian about to leave the wilderness of the world and go to Christ, her lover. The pillar of smoke represents a soul stripped of evil habits, the myrrh denotes mortification of the flesh, frankincense the purity of prayer, and the powdered spices are the other virtues, ground to a fine powder by true contrition.

6 Love's portrait   *Read Song of Songs 4:1–14*

(a) In this long speech, the Bridegroom paints a picture of his virgin love, and verse 7 says it all. Verses 1–5 (part of which is repeated in 6:4–7) and 10–14 fill this out with colourful comparisons in which he lavishes praise on her beauty. Her hair is long, wavy and black (v. 1b) and her graceful neck is adorned with several necklaces one above the other (v. 4), but it is impossible to say what is meant by the references to her eyes (v. 1), breasts (v. 5) or cheeks (v. 14). It is equally difficult to understand the reference in verse 8 to the wilds of the mountain range which forms Israel's northern horizon, except possibly to see here a promise of luxury and security to his love. There are frequent parallels to the 'sister'/'bride' metaphor in ancient Near Eastern love lyrics.

(b) Verses 1–7 comprise a typical *wasf*, a love poem which refers to the beloved's body part by part, using imagery which is both extravagant and sensuous. Others are 5:10–16 and 7:1–7.

(c) Let your imagination play with this picture as a poem of Christ's love for the Church, 'adorned like a bride for her husband' (Revelation 21:2, 9).

These songs can be read as love poems or poems of the love of God. I have tried to illustrate both meanings for each reading. For your meditation I suggest that well-known hymn of Wesley, 'Love divine, all loves excelling, Joy of heaven to earth come down', which speaks about the love of God and is also commonly sung at weddings!

12–18 APRIL   THE SONG OF SONGS 4:15—8:14

1   **Everything in the garden…**   *Read Song of Songs 4:15—5:8*

(a) Here are speeches by the Bride (vv. 15–16), the Bridegroom (5:10) and the Bride again (vv. 2–8).

   In the first two speeches the metaphor of the garden with its running water, lush fruit and cool breezes reminds us of the Garden of Eden. But here there is a significant difference. The climax of the story in Genesis 2–3 is that everyone and everything are at odds, not least the man and the woman. There is enmity between them, and, although the woman still desires the man, the mutuality has gone out of the relationship (Genesis 3:15–16). Here, by contrast, her desire is very real and so is the mutuality of their feelings for each other. Everything in this garden is lovely.

   Things have changed in the Bride's second speech. She dreams of her lover and her dreams are disturbing. It is wonderful when he comes to her, but when her teasing (in verse 3) goes wrong and he goes off, she is distraught. This time her search through the town leads to ridicule. She cries out to the Companions to tell her love that she needs him.

(b) Most commentators see 5:3 to be a lover's tease, though here her lover seems to have lost his sense of humour. As humour adds much to a loving relationship, so the wrong sort of humour can hurt and spoil, especially that 'fun' which is at the other's expense. Here she plays that little bit too hard to get. Others see verses 2–5 as amongst the most sensuous in the whole and read verse 3 as an invitation to her bed.

(c) Here are some examples of 'spiritualizing' readings or meditations which go beyond the plain meaning of the text. Who are these watchmen who strip off the Bride's veil (v. 7)? They are those pagan rulers who strip the martyrs of their flesh, or whose persecution robs the Church of its external clothing when its priests are imprisoned, its altars torn down and its scriptures burned. They are evil spirits who prowl around and strip the faithful of their faith. They are guardian angels or saints who lovingly smite Christian souls with the word of God to strip them of their carnal thoughts or habits.

2 For he is mine and I am his *Read Song of Songs 5:9—6:3*

(a) In this part of the Song, the Companions ask questions (5:9 and 6:1) and the Bride replies (5:10–16 and 6:2–3). Their tone is not mocking but gently teasing and their questions give 'the fairest of women' (cf. 1:8) the opportunity to sing about her 'Beloved'. The search has a happy ending. The lost is found.

Song of Songs 5:10–16 is another love peom (a *wasf*). This one is unusual in that its subject is a man (though there is something of a religious parallel in the description of Onias the High Priest in Ecclesiasticus 50:6–12, to be found in the Apocrypha). She portrays her lover almost as a statue, though here as elsewhere some of the metaphors are lost on us (for example, the doves and the milk in verse 12) and some of the words are guesses (for example, 'palm-fronds' in verse 11). REB's 'fair and desirable' in verse 10 appears as 'white/radiant and *ruddy*' in a number of translations. The Hebrew word translated 'ruddy' (*adom*) is a double pun on the words for 'ground/earth' (*adamah*) and 'man' (*adam* which gives us yet another link with the Garden story in Genesis 2–3 (see Genesis 2:7).

(b) The final verse of this passage, 6:3 ('I am his and he is mine'), repeats 2:16 ('He is mine and I am his') but turns it around. These two verses put together present the ideal of a loving relationship and offer a profound challenge to today's society.

131

come one, but in a unity which fulfils them both. Each
...lers their individualism and receives back their
...uality. Love is a complete mutuality and equality of two
in which neither possesses or dominates the other.

...tors of some Victorian hymnbooks were wary of hymns
which were 'too personal'. They would not have approved of
'Loved with an everlasting love' by the Irish Congregational
minister George Wade Robinson (1838–77). The final verse of
this splendid and now almost totally neglected hymn is heavily
dependent on 6:3:

> *His for ever, only His:*
> *Who the Lord and me shall part?*
> *Ah, with what a rest of bliss*
> *Christ can fill the loving heart!*
> *Heaven and earth may fade and flee,*
> *First-born light in gloom decline;*
> *But, while God and I shall be,*
> *I am His, and He is mine.*

3   She made me a prince   *Read Song of Songs 6:4–12*

(a) She has praised his beauty and in this Bridegroom's song, which
repeats parts of 4:1–3, he sings of her beauty. The poem
continues the royal metaphor—no one in the harem can
compare with his true love. Two verses present real difficulties.

Verse 4 in REB has only two short lines, in which the
Bridegroom compares his love's beauty to the cities of Jerusalem
and Tirzah, the original capital of the northern kingdom before
Samaria replaced it. NRSV and most translations have another
line about 'terrible as an army with banners' or something like
it, which reappears at the end of verse 10. REB has a footnote
saying that the Hebrew adds, 'majestic as the starry heavens',
and this translation appears in verse 10. This meaning is a
possibility, but only one of several. Some commentators suggest
that 'terrible' really means 'terrific', and so her beauty is as
wonderful to see as an army with all its banners. GNB's
'breathtaking' captures that nicely, but it doesn't mention any
armies. 'Hebrew unclear' perhaps says it all.

Verse 12 is widely regarded as the most difficult verse in the Song, and that is some accolade because the competition is stiff! REB makes good sense with, 'I did not recognize myself: she made me a prince chosen from myriads of my people'. He is a nothing and a nobody (v. 11); but his Bride, the fairest of all women and the queen of all queens, has chosen him. Her love makes him feel like a prince. Whether the Hebrew means anything like this is another question. Compare these other two translations:

> 'Before I was aware, my fancy set me
> in a chariot beside my prince' (NRSV—here the Bride is
> speaking).

> 'Before I knew… my desire had hurled me
> onto the chariots of Amminadib' (NJB—the Bridegroom is
> speaking)

Not for nothing does the note 'Hebrew obscure' appear in all the margins here.

(b) 'To love and to cherish' are important words in the wedding service. In verses 4–10 he cherishes her, verbally at least. In REB's translation of verse 12 we see the effect of her cherishing him.

(c) So far, my examples of allegorical readings have been devotional or doctrinal ones. Verses 8–9 have been put to moral use to attack polygamy and defend monogamy.

4   You are my heart's desire   Read Song of Songs 6:13—7:9

(a) Verse 13 is also difficult. The Bride has gone into the garden and the Companions call her back, or possibly ask her to dance (GNB). The Bridegroom takes this as a cue for another description of his Bride's beauty. 'Shulammite' might mean 'Girl of Shulam' (GNB), the village in the Esdraelon valley which was later called Shunem, 'Solomon's girl' or 'Perfect one'; but what lies behind that designation is not clear. Neither is it clear where she moves. Is it between two lines of dancers (REB, NJB) or in the 'Mahanaim dance' (NIV)—whatever that might be—or between two armies (AV, NRSV)?

133

In the rest of this passage in REB the Bridegroom praises her physical beauty, starting from her feet and working upwards. There are no major translation problems but, as before, we cannot follow all the allusions. For seductive sandals, see Judith 16:9 (to be found in the Apocrypha) where the heroine sings of her conquest of Holofernes. What does the compliment about her belly mean (v. 2b)? Does it refer to her nicely rounded tum and its tanned, tawny colour? If so, what about the lilies? Commentators suggest that the allusion is to the custom of storing grain in piles protected by thorn cuttings; but that seems a curious way to store grain! We can see what 'pools of Heshbon' suggests, but why were its reservoirs singled out? And what is special about its Bath-Rabbim gate? That is a question REB readers don't have to ponder, for it translates the phrase as 'crowded city'. The reference to her luxurious black hair in verse 5b may continue the royal metaphor if it is translated as 'a king is held captive in its tresses', as in most translations (though not in REB). In verse 4 we have the last of the Song's allusions to Lebanon. We can't always follow the details but the picture is clear.

(b) There is no mistaking the sensuality of this poem. The Bridegroom celebrates and enjoys his love's body. Verse 9 (and the poem which follows) shows how passionately she responds.

(c) 6:13 and the Shulammite offer endless scope for allegory. In these four 'returns' (REB omits one) the Targum sees that Israel was saved from four oppressors, and some Christians see the four gospels which call Israel to return to God.

5 O perfect love *Read Song of Songs 7:10—8:4*

(a) In REB, the speech of the Bride in 7:10—8:3 is followed by a charge from the Bridegroom (v. 4). The Bride invites her lover out into the countryside. Is it to consummate their love (vv. 10–13)? Even if it is, and that is not certain, it is second best. She yearns for the day when their love will not need to be hidden, and their love-making will be possible under her mother's roof (8:1–3). She yearns for marriage, though saying that she wishes her lover was her brother is a strange way to put it.

The garden imagery we saw at 4:15–16, 5:1, 6:2–3 and 6:11 reappears in verses 10–14. The first part of verse 10 reminds us of 2:16 and 6:3, and the second part takes us straight to the Garden of Eden and Genesis 3:16. The Hebrew word for 'longing' or 'desire' occurs in this sense only in these two places in the Old Testament. Unfortunately REB translates it differently in each place. Mandrakes appear in the Old Testament only here at verse 13 and at Genesis 30:14–16. Both places feature their proverbial aphrodisiac properties.

8:3 repeats 2:6 and pictures the couple in each other's arms. 8:4 repeats 2:7 and many commentators suggest that the editing of the poem is poor here because such a sentiment is simply too late—the couple have already made love. Reading REB as it is, however, could equally suggest that the couple are waiting until the time is ready.

(b) Genesis 3:16 speaks of the woman's desire for the man. Song 7:10 speaks of the man's desire for the woman. Genesis 3:16 says that the power which that gives to the man will be felt as domination, even abuse, by the woman. Song 7:11–12 challenges that sort of relationship between men and women, ancient or modern. It suggests that love's power means giving and liberating rather than taking and controlling.

(c) Reading the Song as a song of God's love to us, there are few more vivid and dynamic descriptions of that love than in the words of the second part of verse 10, that God 'desires' us.

6 Unquenchable *Read Song of Songs 8:5–14*

(a) Commentators do not agree on the divisions between these speeches or on the identity of the speakers. Some think that the poem really ends with verse 7, and NJB actually puts the rest of the chapter in two appendices. Robert Davidson helpfully suggests that this section is like a curtain-call at the end of a play in which each of the three voices has a final say.

REB suggests that it goes something like this. In verse 5a the Companions begin their question in the same way as 3:6, but here they introduce the Bride arriving on the Bridegroom's arm. He has eyes only for his Bride and tells her of the passion of his love (vv. 5b–7). He recognizes that money can't buy her love, and so he offers himself to her as a free gift, but a precious one (seals were among a person's most treasured possessions). The Companions reappear to tease the Bride with a riddle of some kind (vv. 8–9) and she answers them with another (vv. 10–12). Money will not buy her love. She will give it to whom she pleases. The Bridegroom asks if she and the Companions will stop talking in riddles and tell him her decision (v. 13). With the last word she does (v. 14).

(b) On what note should this volume of love poetry close? Those who would end at verse 7, after the three pairs of powerful images in verses 6–7, would end it on a serious and heavy note, for those images speak of the agony and the ecstasy, the passion and the *angst* of love in which lives are made or broken. On the other hand, when I read on to verse 14 I see lightheartedness in the poetry. The Companions tease the Bride with a riddle. She is irrepressible and flings one back at them. The Bridegroom asks, 'What about me?' and off they go together. The humour of this ending says to me that love is a serious business, of course it is; but for love's sake, not that serious!

(c) William Cowper's, 'Hark, my soul! It is the Lord' is a dialogue between God and the human soul. In this verse, based on verses 6–7, God declares his love.

> *Mine is an unchanging love,*
> *Higher than the heights above,*
> *Deeper than the depths beneath,*
> *Free and faithful, strong as death.*

GUIDELINES

(a) On the one hand, the Song of Songs is not easy to read. It is obviously a translation from an ancient and foreign world, no matter how well our modern English Bibles disguise the fact. It is full of dazzling images, rich metaphors and lush descriptions. There are many obscure words and phrases. Even the briefest explanation of these, or of the differences between the REB and any other modern translation, would have taken up more space than is available. On the other hand, because it is a volume of poetry, some of these things don't matter too much. In any case its topic, love—whether the love of God or human love—is one which defies description and definition anyway. If the Song was a treatise on either love in good, plain, straightforward prose, it would not move or excite us in the way that a poem or a hymn can. I hope therefore that you have found reading the Song a joy and a delight as well as a challenge.

(b) The modern way to read the Song is to see it as a collection of love poems, some of which are sexually explicit. Read in this way, it is a celebration of love. Not only that, but also a celebration of youth and of nature. As Robert Davidson puts it, the Song is 'from beginning to end a liberating celebration of human sexuality as something which is good and holy'. God is not mentioned in the Song, yet it echoes with praise for his creation gifts. And not the least of these is that he makes two people into 'one flesh' (Genesis 2:24).

> *Praise God who has created courtship and marriage, joy and gladness, feasting and laughter, pleasure and delight.*

(c) The Old Testament is full of stories of God's love for Israel. The prophet Hosea in particular compares that love to a husband's love for his wife as well as a parent's for his child (2:14–17, 11:1). The Christian faith shares that view of God. Reading the Song of Songs as a hymn of God's love is an ancient way to express our thanksgiving for that love of God which is 'so strong and true, eternal and yet ever new'.

For further reading

R. Davidson, *Ecclesiastes and Song of Solomon*, The Daily Study Bible series, St Andrew Press

Psalms 120–134

The book of Psalms as we now have it in our Bibles is divided into five 'books', reminiscent of the five books of Moses. Within the Psalter, however, there is evidence of earlier collections which have been incorporated into the final edition. One of these collections is the fifteen psalms that comprise the Songs of Ascents.

Within this collection, certain themes predominate. The importance of Jerusalem as a place of pilgrimage is stressed; expressions of confidence, quiet trust and hope abound, despite anxiety and trouble never being far away. In what context might these psalms have been produced? And who are the pilgrims who make their way to the holy city of Jerusalem?

Some commentators think the Songs of Ascents are ancient, and that they reflect aspects of worship at the pilgrimage feasts at Solomon's temple before the exile. Others note the presence in some of the Songs of isolated Aramaic words. This may indicate a date after the exile when Aramaic began to replace Hebrew as a spoken language. A recent study of the Songs of Ascents by Michael Goulder places them at the time of Nehemiah, and links each of them explicitly with Nehemiah's building programme. He thinks they were sung at the Feast of Tabernacles in the year 445BC. It is doubtful whether we can be quite as specific as that, but it may well be that older songs from the time of Solomon's temple were 'recycled' during the second temple period when some of the Jewish people had returned from exile in Babylon.

So as you read these psalms, try to imagine what they might mean to these different people:

- *A farmer and his family from Bethlehem in 715BC. They have made the short trip to Jerusalem once again for one of the pilgrim feasts. How good it is to be surrounded by the familiar hills of Jerusalem, even if the harvest this year was poor and the Assyrian army threatens.*

- *A poor family who have made the long journey from Persia in the year 440BC. Like Nehemiah, their time of exile away from*

the Holy Land is over. They see Jerusalem for the first time,
but face all the dangers of starting afresh in a new land.

• *A Jewish merchant from Rome at the time of Jesus. With his*
  household he is making a once-in-a-lifetime visit to Jerusalem
  for the festival. To be in Jerusalem is a dream come true—as
  is the journey of Muslim pilgrims to Mecca today.

• *A modern Christian reader, who knows that 'here we have no*
  abiding city' (Hebrews 13:14), but nevertheless finds in the
  language of pilgrimage something deep and meaningful. For
  all of us are on pilgrimage and seek 'the city that is to come';
  and so these pilgrim Songs of Ascents continue to speak to the
  heart.

For each of these people, the psalms will have a particular
meaning—the same words, but a new and special resonance.

Quotations are taken from the New Revised Standard Version.

19–25 APRIL   PSALMS 120—126

1   A song in a strange land   *Read Psalm 120*

This is the first of the fifteen psalms which bear the heading 'A
Song of Ascents'. The exact meaning of 'ascents' is disputed. For
our four imagined people, it might mean different things:

For the Bethlehem farmer it might denote the hill country of
Judea. Jerusalem is 'a city set on a hill'. Quite literally you have
to 'go up' in order to reach Jerusalem for the regular festivals.

It would have added meaning for the returning exile. To 'go
up' became a technical term for returning to the homeland. To
this day the term '*Aliyah*', which means 'going up', is used by
Jews returning to the modern state of Israel.

The Jewish merchant from Rome listens to the songs being
sung by the professional singers in the second temple. The
Mishnah, a Jewish law book composed about AD200, relates the
'ascents' to the fifteen steps in the temple leading from the
Court of the Women to the Court of Israel. It therefore
associates the psalm not only with the liturgy but also with the

architecture of Herod's temple in the first century AD.

For today's pilgrim, the meaning may be internalized and spiritualized. In the phrase of the hymn, it may remind us of 'the steep and rugged pathway' in our Christian journey.

At the heart of the complaint in this psalm is the fear of lying lips, false words, deceiving tongues. The power of words to hurt, divide and cause havoc is a common theme in the book of Proverbs, and the letter of James, chapter 3, deals with the disasters produced by the unbridled tongue. Certainly Nehemiah had to face slanderous accusations and malicious gossip in his plan to rebuild Jerusalem.

Meshech and Kedar are two distant areas, one to the north and one to the south of Israel. Meshech (Genesis 10:2) is the name of a tribe occupying land near the Black Sea. Kedar was the second son of Ishmael (Genesis 25:13) and a tribe occupying part of the Arabian desert. Clearly it is geographically impossible to live in both places at once! Perhaps the terms represent the sense of living in the midst of a foreign culture. Both our Persian exile and our Roman merchant would understand these sentiments.

Many modern Christians too may feel misunderstood and misrepresented in the modern world. How often do the media, especially popular 'soap operas', seem to portray Christians in a negative way, gross caricatures of how we perceive ourselves? The sense of being an alien in a hostile land may, therefore, still express a reality for today's pilgrims.

2 God's guardian care *Read Psalm 121*

This lovely psalm of assurance is one of the most popular of the Songs of Ascents. It has offered comfort to pilgrims down the ages. It begins with an opening question and statement from the worshipper (vv. 1–2), followed by words of reassurance and blessing from the officiating priest at the sanctuary (vv. 3–8).

Ancient cities were often built on the tops of hills, where they could be fortified and defended. Jerusalem was no exception, and hills surrounded it on three sides. This still left the city vulnerable from the north, and invading armies such as the

Assyrians, Romans and Crusaders have exploited this weakness. So, the psalmist says, do not look to the hills for help. True help comes from the guardian and protector of his people—only from God himself.

There is no time or place beyond the care of Israel's God, who never slumbers or sleeps. Perhaps there is a deliberate contrast here between Yahweh, the God of Israel, and Baal, the god of the Canaanites. Baal was a fertility god, bringing the rains which made the crops grow. In the Canaanite mythology, which reflects the agricultural cycle, Baal was depicted descending into the underworld during the summer season of drought and subsequently reviving with the coming of the autumn rains. In 1 Kings 18:27 the prophet Elijah on Mount Carmel mocks the unfortunate priests of Baal with the charge that their god is absent, asleep or otherwise engaged! Not so the God of Israel.

The psalm offers words of protection for travellers coming to Jerusalem—and travelling could be hazardous. So our Bethlehem farmer, making the regular journey to the familiar hills, finds comfort. So too do pilgrims of later times and with longer journeys to make in order to reach the holy city. There is protection from sunstroke and also from the baleful influence of the moon (v. 6). In all our coming and going there is no moment, no place, where the pilgrim is out of God's sight. We are under the protection of the all-encompassing love of God, who neither slumbers nor sleeps.

3 Peace to the city of peace   *Read Psalm 122*

Psalm 122 is perhaps the most obvious 'pilgrim psalm' in the whole of the collection. It is also one of a number of 'Zion psalms' in the Psalter—songs which extol the beauty or grandeur of the holy city (see Psalms 46, 48, 76). In the opening two verses the psalmist's delight at being present once again in the city is joyfully expressed. They go to Zion because there, more than anywhere on earth, is to be found the presence of God.

It was David who established Jerusalem as his capital city, and his son Solomon who built the first temple to Yahweh on the site of the Temple Mount. Verses 3–5 extol Jerusalem as a symbol of unity for all Israel and the place from which the royal house rules in righteousness. This would suggest that the psalm comes from the period before 587BC when Jerusalem was destroyed and the last king of Judah deposed by the Babylonians (2 Kings 25). It would seem to have its origin in the time of the first temple, unless the author is looking back and painting an idealistic picture from the more straitened circumstances of the second temple period.

Verses 6–8 pray for peace on the city. In three consecutive verses the word 'shalom' is spoken, a word which means peace, well-being, prosperity and so much more. Perhaps there is a play on the name of the holy city, for Jerusalem means 'city of peace'.

Our four imaginary characters will each recite this psalm and fill it with meaning. The ancient Bethlehem farmer is proud of his city, but knows that great empires like Assyria, Babylon and Egypt threaten its life and existence. The returned exile will learn from bitter experience how precarious life can be in the vulnerable city, as in turn the powers of Persia, Greece and Rome seek world domination. The Roman trader marvels at the glory of Herod's building schemes, including the wonderful temple—but the city is not free; it is under the power of imperial Rome and its governor is Pontius Pilate. Today Jerusalem is still at the centre of turmoil—a place where the Abrahamic faiths of Judaism, Christianity and Islam meet and sometimes clash. The city still needs the prayers of the modern pilgrim for the true welfare of all its citizens. So pray for shalom in Jerusalem, for peace in the city of peace.

4 Lord in your mercy, hear our prayer

Read Psalms 123 and 125

These two brief psalms share common themes. They express a touching confidence in God's goodness, trusting in his mercy at a time of menace and affliction.

Both psalms express their confidence by means of metaphor. As the servant looks to the master or mistress, so we look to God (123:2). As the surrounding hills of the Jerusalem range protect the city, so does God surround his people (125:2). Ultimately the Lord's protecting love is assured.

Yet both psalms hint that all is not well for the pilgrims. They have been at the mercy of 'the contempt of the proud' (123:4) and are menaced by 'those who turn aside to their crooked ways' (125:5). The 'sceptre of wickedness' threatens the welfare of the land (125:3).

From such general references it is difficult to ascertain what the specific problem is. If the psalms are early and pre-exilic, it would indicate the threat from hostile foreign powers to the sovereignty of Israel. It may be preferable, however, to date the psalms later, after the exile. In that case they would reflect the tensions and animosities of the post-exilic period. A number of commentators point to the time of Nehemiah in the mid-fifth century BC. Certainly Nehemiah had to face the 'contempt of the proud' as recorded in Nehemiah 4, where powerful foreign opponents are ranged against him. He also faced internal corruption within the community of returned exiles as depicted in Nehemiah 5. These psalms can be read in terms of external or internal enemies lining up against God's servants. Hence the prayer once again is that 'Peace be upon Israel' (125:5).

So the pilgrims of every age cry for mercy (123:3) and for God's good purposes to be shown (125:4). In Christian liturgy the cry still goes up as it always has, 'Kyrie eleison: Lord, have mercy.'

5 The snare is broken *Read Psalm 124*

Once again, the presence of enemies predominates in this psalm. If it is pre-exilic then the victory may refer to some time of national celebration, such as the defeat of enemy powers. If, however, the psalm comes from after the exile it may refer to some less exalted moment. Nehemiah's 'little local difficulties' may seem small compared to the events of the exodus at the Red Sea or the conquest under Joshua. However, to him they would have seemed just as important as signs of God's providential care.

The poetry of this psalm is particularly evocative. The repetition in verses 1 and 2 is deliberate: it provides emphasis and gives the sense of what a 'near thing' it was. Victory has been snatched from the jaws of defeat only at the last moment, with the help of the Lord.

In verses 3–5 the enemies are vividly portrayed. In verse 3 they are like hungry monsters, their voracious jaws ready to swallow innocent people. It is a common image for destruction and chaos. Indeed *Sheol*, the underworld of Hebrew myth, is depicted with gaping jaws in Proverbs 1:12, and this idea was taken up by the medieval mystery plays in portraying hell. Then in verses 4–5 the picture shifts and the enemies become like raging floodwaters. Once more ancient myth is employed, for chaos was often portrayed as a dark, tempestuous flood. In verses 6–7 the Lord is blessed in a series of short, staccato phrases. The image of bird-traps catching the unwary and innocent is invoked. Yet thanks be to God, 'The snare has been broken and we have escaped'. These are powerful words, and I know of one eucharistic liturgy which uses them as its words of dismissal at the end of the service.

In verse 8 the pilgrims are reminded that the source of their help is in Yahweh the creator of heaven and earth. The language takes us back to Psalm 121.

Whether this psalm celebrates one of the great triumphs of Israel's history or one of the lesser events we shall never know. But it still retains the power to speak to pilgrims today as they face their own moments of personal crisis.

6 Sow in tears, reap with joy *Read Psalm 126*

The desire for a restoration of fortunes lies at the heart of this psalm. Verses 1–3 recall times past when the Lord did great things for his people. Verses 4–6 are a fervent prayer that God will repeat the miracle and come to the aid of his people.

Many commentators link this psalm with the autumn celebrations at the time of the Feast of Tabernacles, which takes place around October. Soon after the festival the early rains should start to fall and the wadis that have long been dry will fill with rushing water. Even those in the far south, the region of the Negeb, will flow with water (v. 4) and new life will spring up in glorious green.

For our Bethlehem farmer, the agricultural images of sowing and reaping would have direct relevance. Once the rains have come and the soil is softened, then the seed can be planted. The seed was often thought to 'die' in the ground, as both Jesus (John 12:24) and Paul (1 Corinthians 15:36) make clear. Sowing may well have been accompanied by rites of mourning and weeping, as it was in surrounding cultures. The contrast with the joy and festivity of harvest could not be greater.

For the returned exiles celebrating Tabernacles in Jerusalem for the first time, the emphasis might be different. Verses 1–3 would remind the family of the joy at the time when the exile ended and Jerusalem began to be restored and the temple rebuilt, to the astonishment of foreign nations. Indeed the AV translates verse 1 as, 'When the Lord turned again the captivity of Zion'. There is still much to be achieved, however, and so the hope and prayer of verses 4–6 swell in the exile's heart: 'Lord, restore our fortunes completely.'

For the visiting merchant from Rome, perhaps the sentiments of the psalm would rekindle the dream that one day the Jewish people would be free of Roman rule, and Zion would stand proud and free once more. At the time of Jesus, Jewish festivals and Jewish nationalism went hand in hand.

For today's Christian pilgrim, the song may bring reminders of harvest festivals and the transformation of the natural order year by year. The words of Jesus and Paul about the seed that must die in order to live may prompt further reflections on the ultimate transformation from death to life—for Jesus and for us. Truly, 'those who sow in tears shall reap with joy'.

GUIDELINES

In imagination we are hearing the Songs of Ascents with the ears of a farmer from Bethlehem in 715BC, a returned exile from Persia in 440BC, a visiting Jewish merchant from Rome in AD30, and a modern Christian reader. Each will hear the same words, but will interpret them differently. In the same way, every reader of *Guidelines* will have their own place and context.

Try now to relate the themes of these psalms to your own spiritual journey. From your own pilgrimage recall a time when:

• *You felt like a stranger in an alien land (Psalm 120)*

- *You needed the shelter of the Keeper of Israel (Psalm 121)*

- *You prayed for the peace of your family, friends or neighbours (Psalm 122)*

- *The cry 'Kyrie eleison/Lord have mercy' was on your lips (Psalms 123 and 125)*

- *You were released to a new freedom (Psalm 124)*

- *Your mouth was filled with laughter (Psalm 126)*

---

26 APRIL–2 MAY   PSALMS 127–134

1   From generation to generation   *Read Psalms 127 and 128*

The themes of prosperity and the gift of children unite these two psalms and encourage us to read them together.

Of all the Songs of Ascents, only Psalm 127 is given a further attribution in the heading as belonging to Solomon. Perhaps the reference to the building of the 'house' in verse 1 encouraged the editors to think of Solomon building the first temple. No doubt after the exile, thoughts would shift rather to the dedication of the second temple in 515BC in the time of Haggai and Zechariah.

It is more likely, however, that the 'house' refers not to the temple as the 'house of God' but rather to the family home. Both psalms rejoice in marriage and family life and once more the psalmists show a liking for the use of simile: children are 'like arrows' (127:4) or 'like olive shoots' (128:3).

No doubt our Bethlehem farmer would have appreciated the importance of the gift of children. The life of an Israelite peasant was hard, the land often stony and unyielding. Many children would mean more hands to work on the land—though, sadly, not all would survive infancy. A large family would ensure that the man's name was passed on to future generations and ownership of the ancestral land was preserved.

The returning exiles from the time of Nehemiah would share the concern for the gift of children. Nehemiah 7:4 informs us that, even when the city wall was completed, the city of

Jerusalem was still under-populated. Nehemiah arranged for one in ten of those living in outlying villages to come and live in the city to boost its population (Nehemiah 11:1–2). The book of Nehemiah also contains long lists of the names of the heads of households and their families who returned to Judah after the exile was over.

Later readers may interpret these psalms in a more domestic way. It has been suggested that Psalm 127 is a psalm to be sung after the birth of a child. Martin Luther described Psalm 128 as a marriage song. Today, on a global scale, we are more concerned about over-population than under-population. Family sizes in western Europe and the USA have fallen sharply. Some countries have tried to restrict the size of families. Still, for all that, readers in many parts of the world will share the sentiments of these psalms, and look for the prosperity of their community as they celebrate the birth of a child.

2 Furrowed backs—and defiance   *Read Psalm 129*

In many ways this is a rather curious psalm. It does not really fit any of the common types or forms of psalm. Perhaps it comes nearest to a kind of national lament. However, the themes are typical of the Songs of Ascents. Familiar phrases are repeated, such as 'let Israel now say' (see also 124:1), and use is made of metaphor and simile.

In some ways this psalm is similar to Psalm 126, in that it is neatly divided into two halves. However, it presents the negative side rather than the positive features of the earlier psalm. Whereas verses 1–3 of Psalm 126 recounted the famous saving exploits of the Lord, verses 1–4 of Psalm 129 rehearse the dismal episodes in Israel's troubled history. As 'the cockpit of the middle east', Israel was often brutally subject to the tramping of armies across the land. So whereas the second half of Psalm 126 called on God to restore the good fortunes of the nation, the second half of Psalm 129 calls down curses on the opponents of Zion.

For the Bethlehem farmer, these opponents might be the armies of the king of Assyria which menaced the land of Israel.

If the psalm comes from the time of Nehemiah, then those hostile to the holy city could be identified with the likes of Sanballat, Tobiah and Geshem, who opposed the rebuilding of the city (Nehemiah 6).

In fact, the history of oppression suffered by the Jewish people down the ages means that the designation in verse 5, 'all who hate Zion', takes on a different meaning in each succeeding generation, including our own century of anti-Semitism.

No one would contend that Psalm 129 is the prettiest or most profound of the Songs of Ascents. Nevertheless, as so often with the Psalms, its sentiments are real and its emotions raw. If we are honest, there are times when we feel the same, and then the psalm can speak for us.

3   Out of the depths   *Read Psalm 130*

The Latin title of this psalm is *De Profundis*, 'Out of the Depths'. It is indeed a psalm which speaks from and to the depths of the human condition. It speaks of the universal sinfulness of humanity and also of the merciful, saving love of God. It was a favourite psalm of Martin Luther who made connections between its words and those of the gospels and the letters of Paul. In 1523 Luther wrote one of his greatest hymns based on the words of this psalm: 'Out of the depths I cry to thee, Lord God. O hear my prayer.'

The psalm is very personal, but it is not purely individualistic. The speaker may be a representative figure who speaks for the whole congregation. Before the exile it may have been the king himself; after the exile, when the kingship no longer existed, the words may have been spoken by a priest. The psalm ends with words of encouragement addressed to the whole congregation in verses 7–8.

Certain poetic devices are used which are typical of the Songs of Ascents. The use of repetition for emphasis in verse 6 is similar to that in Psalms 124 and 129. The language of waiting patiently and hoping confidently are typical of the collection. The phrase 'O Israel, hope in the Lord!' in verse 7 recurs in the following Psalm 131.

The themes of this psalm are profound but the language itself is very general. This is typical of the psalms and it is difficult to know exactly what the danger is. The advantage of this is that the psalm is capable of being used in private or public for all kinds of situations. Each of our pilgrims will apply it to their own circumstances. This is exactly what Luther did in the crises he faced in the 1520s. The psalm still speaks to us, 'out of the depths'.

4 David's vow to God   *Read Psalm 132:1–10*

This psalm recalls the events described in 2 Samuel 6, in which David arranges for the ark of the covenant to be brought to Jerusalem as its final resting place. However, David's plans to build a temple to house the ark have to be 'put on hold' (2 Samuel 7). His son Solomon will eventually order the construction of the temple (1 Kings 6–8).

Psalm 132 seems not only to retell the story but actually to relive it. Some commentators think that drama was an important part of worship in the temple. If that is correct, then this psalm may have been used as part of a procession which recreated the story each year. This would have been in the autumn at the Feast of Tabernacles, for that was when the original temple was dedicated (1 Kings 8:2). Whether the sacred ark was brought out of the temple and processed around the city we do not know, but it seems possible that the story of David and the ark was re-enacted in some way. The author of the book of Chronicles quotes verses 8–10 of this psalm in his later retelling of the Samuel/Kings story (see 2 Chronicles 6:41–42).

Of all the Songs of Ascents this is the one most likely to be from the early pre-exilic period. When the Babylonians captured the city and destroyed the temple in 587BC, the precious ark of the covenant was lost. There is a legend preserved in one of the books of the Apocrypha that the ark was taken and hidden by Jeremiah until the time God would reveal it again (2 Maccabees 2:4–8). Despite the vivid imagination of Hollywood in the film *Raiders of the Lost Ark*, the sacred covenant box, the footstool of God himself, has never been found!

Perhaps our Bethlehem farmer would have taken part in the ceremonies and watched the procession. Perhaps his chest would have swelled with pride at the mention of Ephrathah in verse 6, for this was another name for the Bethlehem region where David and his ancestors were born (Ruth 4:11). For those of later times there were no processions to watch. The hearts of our Persian exile and merchant from Rome could still be stirred by this psalm; for they heard again the old story proclaimed in song, and remembered that one day a new ruler would arise from Bethlehem Ephrathah (Micah 5:2).

5 God's vow to David *Read Psalm 132:11–18*

After relating the story of the ark being brought to Jerusalem (2 Samuel 6), chapter 7 continues by telling of David's intention to build a 'house' for God, a holy temple in the city. Instead of this, God makes a vow to David to build him a 'house' by securing the dynasty of David. That vow is reflected in this psalm. Verses 1–10 concentrate on David's vow, while the second half of the psalm reflects on God's promises to David.

Verses 11–18 are an oracle, perhaps spoken by a temple prophet or priest. They restate in fairly traditional language the promises of the Lord to David and his heirs. His sons will sit on the throne in Jerusalem just as God is enthroned in Zion. The king is God's representative on earth and through him the Lord will bless his needy people and defeat their enemies.

However, the promise is not unconditional. Verse 12 spells out the conditions: 'If your sons keep my covenant…'—which, of course, they did not, so that Jerusalem fell and the kings of David's line failed. Yet still this psalm was preserved and sung in the period of the second temple, as a new context brought new meaning. Our farmer in the year 715BC would associate the psalm with good King Hezekiah, who sat on his ancestor David's throne. For those hearing the psalm in 440BC or AD30 the words become prophetic and anticipatory. Yes, in 440 the wall of Jerusalem had been rebuilt by Nehemiah and its houses and temple were secure; but still there was no king in Jerusalem. Nehemiah himself was only a governor. Certainly, in AD30 the huge building programme of Herod the Great and his successors had splendidly rebuilt the temple and the city. The temple buildings were more magnificent than they had ever been. Yet Herod was not of David's line. So Psalm 132:17 speaks seditiously of an anointed one in this new temple, a lamp prepared, a horn that would sprout. One day there would again be a true descendent of David, a Messiah.

Modern Christian readers will also read this psalm messianically, but will apply it to the Messiah who has come—to Jesus. In the words of the hymn, the psalm will speak to us of 'Great David's greater Son'.

6   The pilgrims depart   *Read Psalms 131, 133 and 134*

Three short psalms bring the collection to a close. They are even shorter than usual among the Songs of Ascents. With them the pilgrims prepare to depart from the temple as the Feast of Tabernacles draws to a close.

Psalm 131: A beautiful, intimate psalm which is a real treasure amongst this collection. Despite distress and troubles, the psalmist has a genuine sense of peace. Children were usually weaned on to solid food by about three years of age. Though the child no longer needed the mother's milk, there was still comfort to be found on the mother's lap. So the psalmist has learned to put aside all arrogance and haughtiness, and to become like a little child (see Mark 10:14–15). The soul can rest secure, safe in the mothering love of God.

Psalm 133: The Feast of Tabernacles in every age was a time to foster unity. Old friends were seen again by the regular visitors to Jerusalem, while newcomers found new friends in the cultic community celebrations. Old enmities were forgotten at the start of the new year. All this is portrayed in this psalm and, once again, the use of simile is to the fore. High priests from Aaron onwards were anointed with olive oil. The oil was a symbol of the grace and favour of God. Hermon was the highest mountain in the area, on the far northern borders of Israel. So 'dew of Hermon' was probably a proverbial expression.

Psalm 134: Imagine that it is the last night of the Feast of Tabernacles. The Bethlehem farmer is ready to return to his fields a few miles away. He will be back for the next festival. The merchant from Rome will go back to his trading, never to see the holy city again. Psalm 134 is an evening psalm which concludes the Songs of Ascents. The congregation addresses the priests in verses 1–2 and asks them to bless the Lord with hands outstretched towards the sanctuary. In verse 3 the priests respond, turning to the assembled congregation with a final benediction. Their blessing captures the essence of the Songs of Ascents. The maker of heaven and earth (Psalm 121:2) who graciously dwells enthroned in Zion (Psalm 132:13) will bless his pilgrim people as they journey home.

GUIDELINES

We have tried to stand in the shoes of four pilgrims, both ancient and modern. We have attempted to listen with their ears and to walk with them on their pilgrim way to Zion. They each hear the same words of these brief Songs of Ascents, but each interprets the meaning in the light of their own experience and situation. Their understanding is governed by the time and place in which they live. This is hardly surprising. A congregation on any Sunday morning will all hear the same words of a sermon, but each one will appreciate different aspects of the preacher's message. Often preachers might be surprised to discover what the members of the congregation thought they had said!

Try once again to apply the truths of these psalms to your own pilgrim journey, remembering especially times of patience, hope, anger, desolation, promise and contentment. Use them also to pray for others:

- *for families you know and care about (Psalms 127 and 128)*
- *for those who are suffering and angry (Psalm 129)*
- *for those in the depths of despair (Psalm 130)*
- *for young children and all they can teach us (Psalm 131)*
- *for those who rule or govern others (Psalm 132)*

- *for your closest friends (Psalm 133)*

- *for all ministers, priests, servants of the Lord (Psalm 134)*

    Lord, give me the heart of a pilgrim. Teach me to sing the songs of Zion and guide my feet to go up the pilgrim way. So may I, at last, stand in your presence and never more depart. Amen.

Further reading

Two recent studies focus particularly on the Songs of Ascents, both looking at the Songs as a coherent whole and placing them in the wider context of the book of Psalms.

Michael Goulder, *The Psalms of the Return*, Sheffield Academic Press, 1998. This argues for the Songs of Ascents being specifically linked with the historical period of Nehemiah.

David C. Mitchell, *The Message of the Prophets*, Sheffield Academic Press, 1997. This relates the Songs not so much to historical events but rather to the future hopes (eschatology) of the post-exilic period. They reflect the outlook of later prophecy and are future-oriented.

For a general survey of the book of Psalms see John Day, *Psalms*, Old Testament Guides, Sheffield Academic Press, 1992.

The Bible Reading Fellowship
Peter's Way, Sandy Lane West, Oxford, OX4 5HG
ISBN 1 84101 011 1

Distributed in Australia by:
Hodder Headline Australia, 10–16 South Street,
Rydalmere, (Locked Bag 386), NSW 2116

Distributed in New Zealand by:
Scripture Union Wholesale, PO Box 760, Wellington

Distributed in South Africa by:
Struik Book Distributors, PO Box 193, Maitland 7405

Publications distributed to more than 60 countries

Acknowledgments
The Revised Standard Version of the Bible, copyright ©
1946, 1952, 1971 by the Division of Christian Education
of the National Council of the Churches of Christ in the
USA.

The New Revised Standard Version of the Bible, copyright ©
1989 by the Division of Christian Education of the
National Council of the Churches of Christ in the USA.

The Holy Bible, New International Version, copyright ©
1973, 1978, 1984 by International Bible Society.

New English Bible copyright © 1970 by permission of
Oxford and Cambridge University Presses.

Revised English Bible copyright © 1989, by permission of
Oxford and Cambridge University Presses.

Printed in Denmark

SUBSCRIPTIONS

NEW DAYLIGHT–GUIDELINES–LIVEWIRES

Our subscription rates remain unchanged for 1999–2000:

Individual subscriptions covering 3 issues for under 5 copies, payable in advance (including postage and packing):

		UK	surface	airmail
LIVEWIRES (8–10 yr olds)	3 volumes p.a.	£12.00	£13.50	£15.00
GUIDELINES	each set of 3 p.a.	£9.60	£10.80	£13.20
NEW DAYLIGHT	each set of 3 p.a.	£9.60	£10.80	£13.20
NEW DAYLIGHT LGE PRINT	each set of 3 p.a.	£15.00	£18.60	£21.00

Group subscriptions covering 3 issues for 5 copies or more, sent to ONE address (post free):

LIVEWIRES	£10.50	3 volumes p.a.
GUIDELINES	£8.10	each set of 3 p.a.
NEW DAYLIGHT	£8.10	each set of 3 p.a.
NEW DAYLIGHT LGE PRINT	£13.50	each set of 3 p.a.

Please note that the annual billing period for Group Subscriptions runs from 1 May to 30 April.

Copies of the notes may also be obtained from Christian bookshops:

LIVEWIRES	£3.50 each copy
GUIDELINES and NEW DAYLIGHT	£2.70 each copy
NEW DAYLIGHT LGE PRINT	£4.50 each copy

Please note that the Lightning Bolts range also includes volumes of undated daily Bible reading notes for 10–14 year olds. Contact your local bookshop or BRF direct for details.

SUBSCRIPTIONS

❑ I would like to give a gift subscription (please complete both name and
  address sections below)
❑ I would like to take out a subscription myself (complete name and
  address details only once)
❑ Please send me details of 3-year subscriptions

This completed coupon should be sent with appropriate payment to BRF.
Alternatively, please write to us quoting your name, address, the subscription you
would like for either yourself or a friend (with their name and address), the start
date and credit card number, expiry date and signature if paying by credit card.

Gift subscription name _____

Gift subscription address _____

_____ Postcode _____

Please send to the above, beginning with the May 1999 issue:

(please tick box)	UK	SURFACE	AIR MAIL
LIVEWIRES	❑ £12.00	❑ £13.50	❑ £15.00
GUIDELINES	❑ £9.60	❑ £10.80	❑ £13.20
NEW DAYLIGHT	❑ £9.60	❑ £10.80	❑ £13.20
NEW DAYLIGHT LARGE PRINT	❑ £15.00	❑ £18.60	❑ £21.00

Please complete the payment details below and send your coupon, with
appropriate payment to: **The Bible Reading Fellowship, Peter's Way, Sandy
Lane West, Oxford OX4 5HG**

Your name _____

Your address _____

_____ Postcode _____

Total enclosed £ _____ (cheques should be made payable to 'BRF')

Payment by cheque ❑ postal order ❑ Visa ❑ Mastercard ❑ Switch ❑

Card number: ❏❏❏❏ ❏❏❏❏ ❏❏❏❏ ❏❏❏❏

Expiry date of card: ❏❏❏❏   Issue number (Switch): ❏❏❏❏

Signature (essential if paying by credit/Switch card) _____

NB: BRF notes are also available from your local Christian bookshop.

GL0199   The Bible Reading Fellowship is a Registered Charity

BIBLE READING RESOURCES PACK

A pack of resources and ideas to help to promote Bible reading in your church is available from BRF. The pack which will be of use at any time during the year includes sample editions of the notes, magazine articles, leaflets about BRF Bible reading resources and much more. Unless you specify the month in which you would like the pack sent, we will send it immediately on receipt of your order. We greatly appreciate your donations towards the cost of producing the pack (without them we would not be able to make the pack available) and we welcome your comments about the contents of the pack and your ideas for future ones.

This coupon should be sent to:

The Bible Reading Fellowship
Peter's Way
Sandy Lane West
Oxford OX4 5HG

Name _____

Address _____

_____

_____ Postcode _____

Please send me _____ Bible Reading Resources Pack(s)

Please send the pack now/ in_____ (month).

I enclose a donation for £_____ towards the cost of the pack.

This page is intentionally left blank

BRF PUBLICATIONS ORDER FORM

Please ensure that you complete and send off both sides of this order form.
Please send me the following book(s):

		Quantity	Price	Total
032	Message for the Millennium (D. Winter)	_____	£5.99	_____
3565	Sometimes the Donkey is Right (B. Ogden)	_____	£3.25	_____
3566	Best Friends (B. Ogden)	_____	£3.25	_____
018	Shepherds and Angels (B. Ogden)	_____	£3.25	_____
019	Too Busy to Listen (B. Ogden)	_____	£3.25	_____

Total cost of books £ _____

Postage and packing (see over) £ _____

TOTAL £ _____

See over for payment details. All prices are correct at time of going to press, are subject to the prevailing rate of VAT and may be subject to change without prior warning.
NB: All BRF titles are also available from your local Christian bookshop.

GL0199   The Bible Reading Fellowship is a Registered Charity

PAYMENT DETAILS

Please complete the payment details below and send with appropriate payment and completed order form to:

The Bible Reading Fellowship,
Peter's Way,
Sandy Lane West,
Oxford OX4 5HG

Name _____

Address _____

_____

_____Postcode _____

Total enclosed £ _____ (cheques should be made payable to 'BRF')

Payment by cheque ❏ postal order ❏ Visa ❏ Mastercard ❏ Switch ❏

Card number: ☐☐☐☐ ☐☐☐☐ ☐☐☐☐ ☐☐☐☐

Expiry date of card: ☐☐☐☐ Issue number (Switch): ☐☐☐☐

Signature (essential if paying by credit/Switch card) _____

POSTAGE AND PACKING CHARGES			
order value	UK	Europe	Surface	Air Mail
£7.00 & under	£1.25	£2.25	£2.25	£3.50
£7.01–£14.99	£3.00	£3.50	£4.50	£6.50
£15.00–£29.99	£4.00	£5.50	£7.50	£11.00
£30.00 & over	free	prices on request		

Alternatively you may wish to order books using the BRF telephone order hotline:
01865 748227

The Bible Reading Fellowship is a Registered Charity